FOR THOSE AT RISK . . .

The information in this book is for you and your loved ones!

Anyone, regardless of age, sex or ethnic background, can develop a high cholesterol level without even being aware of it. Are you one of the many individuals who has or is at risk for developing cardiovascular disease?

This book:

A. Enables you to understand and work more easily with your physician in lowering and controlling your cholesterol.

B. Is a guide for having your cholesterol level checked and helping you understand the results.

C. Enables you to be successful in lowering your cholesterol level, if necessary, in the easiest way and the shortest period of time.

D. Helps you understand some basic information about your own body chemistry and its relationship to the foods you eat and their relationship to cholesterol.

E. Explains the relationship of cholesterol to cardiovascular diseases.

Lowering your cholesterol level is a personal affair. Only through personal initiative, understanding your body chemistry and following a proper program can your cholesterol level be controlled.

The information in this book is not for self diagnosing but does enable you to work more effectively with your doctor. Physicians do recommend this book.

Children should not be placed on a low fat, low cholesterol diet unless prescribed by their physician. Children in their early years require a moderate amount of fat for proper development.

> Your heart, a muscle the size of your fist,
> beats about 100,000 times per day while
> pumping approximately 2,000 gallons of blood
> through 12,400 miles of blood vessels.

Cholesterol
LOWERING and CONTROLLING
3 WEEK PLAN
HANDBOOK and COOKBOOK

Patricia T. Krimmel
Edward A. Krimmel

Preface by
David M. Capuzzi, M.D., Ph.D.

Foreword by
Robert H. Bendy, Jr., M.D.

Illustrator,
Art & Design Editor
Charles A. Krimmel

FRANKLIN PUBLISHERS

Box 1338
Bryn Mawr, PA 19010

PUBLICATIONS AVAILABLE
FROM FRANKLIN PUBLISHERS

The following items may be ordered directly from
Franklin Publishers, Box 1338, Bryn Mawr, PA 19010.
Write for current prices. Quantity discounts are available.

- **THE LOW BLOOD SUGAR HANDBOOK**—by Edward and Patricia
  Krimmel. Highly praised by Harvey Ross, M.D., this is a new upscaled
  approach to the diagnosis and treatment of hypoglycemia (low blood
  sugar), written with the insight and practicality that only a sufferer
  could have, but backed up by meticulous research and medical
  accuracy. The book of solutions! 192 pages
- **THE LOW BLOOD SUGAR COOKBOOK**—by Patricia and Edward
  Krimmel. A very special collection of over 200 sugarless natural food
  recipes. Snacks to gourmet dishes designed specifically for the
  hypoglycemic, but which everyone can enjoy and are also valuable to
  diabetics and weight watchers. No artificial sweeteners or white flour
  are used in the recipes. Only fruit and fruit juices are used as
  sweeteners. 192 pages
- **ONE (1) HOUR LOW BLOOD SUGAR CASSETTE**—A dynamic
  presentation by the authors of THE LOW BLOOD SUGAR
  HANDBOOK, Ed & Pat Krimmel. Get the feeling of personal contact
  with the authors when hearing an interview followed by a question
  and answer session.
- **THE CHOLESTEROL LOWERING AND CONTROLLING 3 WEEK
  PLAN: HANDBOOK & COOKBOOK**—by Patricia and Edward
  Krimmel. See order form in back of book.
- **CHOLESTEROL LOWERING COOKBOOK**—By Patricia and Edward
  Krimmel. See page 118 or 248.

Franklin Publishers
P.O. Box 1338
Bryn Mawr, PA 19010

Library of Congress Catalog No. 89-84777   First Edition

ISBN 0-916503-03-8   Printed in the U.S.A.

CONTENTS

PREFACE

By David M. Capuzzi, M.D., Ph.D.

Dr. Capuzzi is Director of the Lipid Disorders Center, Professor of Medicine and Biochemistry, Medical College of Pennsylvania; Associate in Medicine, Lankenau Hospital, and Adjunct Professor of Medicine and Biochemistry, Thomas Jefferson University, Philadelphia, Pennsylvania. He is the author of numerous research papers on lipids and lipoproteins.

Over the past five years, the public has been deluged with a mass of information from both health organizations and the news media concerning the issues of blood cholesterol control and cardiovascular disease risk. A variety of medical studies have been cited to support various points of view. The public has received the message that something can and should be done to lower the risk for heart attack, but that medical authorities disagree on the best approaches to take. The resulting controversies have led to confusion and skepticism compounded by the vigorous promotion of various remedies to lower blood cholesterol. A number of questions have been raised: Does sufficient scientific information exist to warrant implementation of measures to lower blood cholesterol levels? Should these measures be applied to the overall population or only to those at high risk? How should age and sex factors be considered in formulating medical evaluation and treatment plans? Do the benefits of lowering blood cholesterol outweigh the issues of safety, efficacy, expense, and inconvenience of various treatment modalities?

While it is important for Medicine to question its hypotheses in the light of new information, it is essential that the public receive adequate and accurate information. The National Cholesterol Education Program has been launched to educate both health care professionals and the public about steps that should be taken to lower coronary disease risk. Coronary atherosclerosis is a complex disease. There are no easy absolute answers to its relationship to cholesterol metabolism, and to the interplay of hereditary and environmental influences. However, through a careful, critical review of the enormous body of available medical evidence, a number of reasoned conclusions can be reached:

- The evidence linking high blood cholesterol in a causal fashion with increased risk of premature development of coronary heart disease is overwhelming and unassailable.
- A host of biochemical, genetic, nutritional, epidemiologic, and clinical studies carried out over the past 50 years support this relationship in a consistent fashion.
- The higher the blood cholesterol level, the greater the coronary risk.
- Intake of a high cholesterol, high saturated fat, calorie-rich diet is a major contributing factor to high blood cholesterol levels and increased coronary risk.
- Other risk factors such as a family history of premature coronary heart disease, cigarette smoking, the presence of hypertension, diabetes mellitus, excessive weight, sedentary lifestyle, and stress increase the absolute risk imparted by high blood cholesterol.
- Lowering of elevated blood cholesterol levels by prudent, sustained intake of healthful foods, and the judicious use of medications under medical supervision can reduce one's risk for coronary events such as heart attack.
- Reduction or removal of other modifiable risk factors at any given cholesterol level is beneficial, and should be part of a treatment plan.

The benefits from blood cholesterol-lowering appear to be greatest in those who are at increased cardiovascular risk for other reasons. However, there is individual variation in response to treatment and there is no unqualified assurance of a health advantage for every individual who undertakes such measures. Therefore, there is no substitute for evaluation by a physician capable of assessing carefully the cause and risk of blood cholesterol elevation in a given individual. The physician can then decide upon prudent intervention measures, and recommend a safe, cholesterol-lowering regimen that may improve the patient's health.

Considerable patient education is usually needed to accomplish the goals of therapy. Suitable reading material should be provided as a valuable adjunct to a treatment program. At present, there is an extensive body of literature available. In this book, the Krimmels focus on sound basic principles, in a clear and readable format. Sufficient background material is given on cholesterol metabolism and arterial plaque development without overburdening the reader. The authors have emphasized the importance of utilizing simple tools to reach achievable goals with appropriate health care supervision. This book can supplement the patient's basic knowledge while under the care of a physician, and provide a valuable primer on this subject. The recipes can be utilized or modified to suit personal food preferences and to complement dietary information obtained from a physician. The recent guidelines for blood cholesterol-lowering provided by the National Cholesterol Education Program correctly underscore restricted intake of dietary cholesterol, saturated fat, and calories as initial measures to achieve a lowered blood cholesterol level. A diet tailored to suit individual tastes and needs over a long term is essential. The future holds promise for further advances in this field and exciting improvements in therapy—but a prudent diet will remain its cornerstone. The Krimmels have provided an interesting and timely addition to the available literature in this important health area of cardiac risk reduction.

We dedicate this book to:

You, the reader.

Everyone who is interested in his/her well-being.

Those brave people who are willing to think about their body chemistry and modify their behavior so they will have more healthful and fulfilling lives.

To Helen, Taylor, Rose and George, our Parents, in loving memory of their goodness.

The memory of Bob, Al and John.

To all our loved ones.

To the glory of the Lord and may all things be done with the understanding of the Word.

ACKNOWLEDGMENTS

Our special thanks to the individuals who made a valuable contribution to this book, whether by lending an ear, reading the manuscript, making suggestions or testing recipes. We could never have completed this book without the help and assistance of Ethel Young, Lewis and Celia Creskoff, Dan and Connie Rondeau, Peter and Susan Robinson, John and Betty Aukstikalnes, Bob and Irene Bendy, David Capuzzi, Susan Thomas, Frank Colgan, Frank Smith and Charles Atkinson.

Take a Chance

There's someone for everyone,
And a place in life too.
You can be anything,
Accept no handicaps,
Settle for nothing but the best.
It's yours for the taking,
Never give up,
Never give in.
Don't let others bring you down,
Strive,
Survive,
And Never be afraid,
To take a chance.

Welcome to: The Essence of Me
Dan G. Smith, Poet, Chula Vista, CA

FOREWORD

By Robert H. Bendy, Jr., M.D.

Dr. Bendy is Attending Physician, Department of Internal Medicine at the Mountainside Hospital, Montclair, New Jersey. In private practice he concentrates on Immunologic Disorders and Metabolic, Dietary Diseases in relation to Coronary Artery Heart Disease.

The Center for Disease Control estimates that sixty million Americans are candidates for medical intervention of control of high cholesterol. The Second Interventional Conference on Preventive Cardiology at the annual meeting of the American Heart Association Council stunned the world's medical leaders by revealing that hypercholesteremia in relation to its causative effect on cardiovascular morbidity and mortality is virtually a world epidemiologic crisis because of its astounding association as a singular risk factor in heart attack and stroke.

Some of the sources in periodical medical information, from the Helsinki Heart Study to the Framingham, Mass. Population Study, demonstrated seemingly immune individuals to this world wide killer. This has caused more attention to a single substance than anything in world medical experience.

Cholesterol! You hear it on the streets. Patients no longer whisper about it in my waiting room. Everyone is asking, "What is my cholesterol number?" We know this is not a simple question, nor is there a simple solution. Doctors are telling you the best test now available to determine risk factor is a Lipid Profile. They'll talk of abbreviated terms such as your LDL, HDL, and VLDL, and when they have related these figures to you, do nothing more, it

11

seems, than put you on a strict, low fat diet. They will tell you to eat no more than 30% fat, all of which should be "mono and/or polyunsaturated." Dietitians will advise against eating too much animal fat, but in the same breath, they seemingly contradict their statement by telling you to eliminate all tropical oils such as coconut and palmates.

By now, I am sure that none of this material makes any sense at all, but consider this fact stated in an issue of Preventive Cardiology, "There is a desperate need to develop policy for controlling the coronary epidemic. Reducing the impact where it is already raging and prevent it from becoming a raging problem in developing countries." The dilemma occurs when considering the only treatment recommended is aggressive dietary change, and the need for knowledge with more vigorous appreciation of our current status. The Health Education Foundation for Prevention and Control of Cardiovascular Disease has been supplying literature and guidelines for physicians and patients over the past decade on the identification of those at risk and how to treat this becomes more complex daily.

Total dietary modification for reducing cholesterol and related fats in one's diet obviously for now is agreed upon to be the number one factor of importance, and at this most auspicious time, we find Ed and Pat Krimmel, authors of the Low Blood Sugar Handbook on the scene with the needed information to help one understand the dietary food groups, cholesterol and its other associated substances in an easy to read text with an accompanying cookbook.

Just as they took you by the hand through the maze of the complicated vocabulary associated with low blood sugar, they will lead you step by step into the world of cholesterol, hyperlipidemia, dyslipidemias, and then explain each in an easy to read fashion. Their expertise and teaching methods, along with true concern for this world health problem, is certainly admirable. They are to be commended on the lengthy hours of research and commitment to excellence.

We are all concerned with life and our own physical well being. Whether you have a cholesterol problem or not; even if you have never had a test ordered by a doctor to determine your lipid profile; you will not want to wait to begin the text of this timely publication. It is relevant to everyone. The Krimmels have made it exciting to be involved in this continuing educational project.

Strange World

It's a strange world,
Full of strange people.
People wandering the streets,
People searching for themselves.
People killing one another,
People helping one another.
Friends shaking hands,
Enemies striking blows.
Wanting to fit in,
Wanting to be different.
Rich,
Bankrupt.
Kind,
Cruel.
Yes it is a strange world,
And I'm part of it.

Welcome to: The Essence of Me
Dan G. Smith, Poet, Chula Vista, CA

Charles Krimmel

1

UNDERSTANDING CHOLESTEROL

If you think the issue of cholesterol is hot and or new, let's just get a few facts from medical history straight and current. As early as 1908, a Russian researcher by the name of Ignatowsky fed rabbits meat, milk and eggs for several months. He discovered that their aortas (largest artery) developed arteriosclerotic lesions. The lesions contained deposits of lipids and cholesterol and closely resembled the arteriosclerotic lesions found in humans. For the first time, it was shown that arteriosclerosis could be induced by the foods one ate, dispelling the idea that arteriosclerosis had an infectious origin. However Ignatowsky's findings gave rise to another misconception—that arteriosclerosis was a disease of protein intoxication.

Another Russian researcher, Anitschkow, thought that the cholesterol in the lesions might have come from the cholesterol in the food the rabbits were fed. He and his associate fed rabbits purified cholesterol and discovered that the rabbits developed high blood cholesterol as well as deposits of lipids and cholesterol in their liver, spleen, arteries and other tissues. The lesions in the arteries contained abundant lipids and cholesterol. From his results, Anitschkow concluded that cholesterol in food could induce arteriosclerosis.

In 1916 the Dutch physician DeLangen believed high blood cholesterol levels increased the incidence of atherosclerosis and gall stones among Javanese people working on Dutch ships. Both of these conditions were rare among native Javanese, but those who ate the meat and dairy foods of the rich Dutch diet developed high blood cholesterol and arteriosclerosis.

Since these early discoveries, much more has been learned about cholesterol. In 1968, research established that the cholesterol in the plaque in the arteries comes from the LDL cholesterol in the blood stream.

What may be even more important, additional research has unequivocally proven that eating saturated fat makes blood cholesterol rise more than eating cholesterol itself.

Because research continues, you must keep abreast of the new information available and actively seek out the information.

In order for you to grasp the concepts related to blood cholesterol and its relationship to your overall body chemistry, you must do two things:

1. Learn a few new terms and the relationship of these terms to your body chemistry.
2. Be patient while trying to learn, understand, and apply the information.

To lower and control your cholesterol, you do not need to learn all of the scientific information related to cholesterol. However, it is sometimes easier to do something if you understand the real reasons for what you are doing. You be the judge of how far you want to delve into the scientific information.

To help you understand the technical terms contained in the text, you may find it helpful to refer to the glossary located in the back of the book. Understanding the terms is very important for your being able to learn the concepts which are necessary for your long term progress. We tried to keep the new terms to a minimum.

CHOLESTEROL, A VITAL PART OF YOUR BODY CHEMISTRY

In recent years cholesterol has been under heavy attack. It seems every authority, except for the local dog catcher, has been giving it a bad rap. The truth of the matter is cholesterol is essential and very much needed for the cells in your body. However, just as any good thing, when there is too much of it, it can cause serious health problems.

WHAT IS CHOLESTEROL AND WHERE DOES IT COME FROM?

Cholesterol is a soft, odorless, waxy-type substance which is part of all animal cells, including those of human's. It is one of a number of fats, called lipids, found in the blood.

There are two primary sources of cholesterol:

1. Within the body—the liver, intestine and skin produce all the cholesterol the body needs.
2. In foods we eat—foods only of animal origin such as:
   egg yolks
   dairy products
   meats, fish, poultry
   The cholesterol content of meat is found mostly in the lean tissue not the fat. A food may contain substantial cholesterol but only a moderate amount of fat (for example, an egg yolk has only 6 gms. of fat but 210 mgs. of cholesterol). Foods of plant origin have no cholesterol.

The amount of cholesterol produced by the body is determined by your body chemistry and possibly by the amount of cholesterol you eat. It may be that for some people, the more cholesterol eaten the less the body produces but this connection has not yet been proven.

WHY DO WE NEED CHOLESTEROL?

Cholesterol is essential to many of the body's chemical processes. Some examples are:

- Is a key substance in the walls of every cell
- Is an aid in hormone production
- Is essential for brain and nerve development
- Is the starting material from which the liver produces bile acids which are necessary for the digestion of fats
- Is the precursor for production of steroid hormones by the adrenal glands and gonads

Remember, since your body can manufacture all of the cholesterol it needs, you may not need to consume any additional amounts. It is, however, unnecessary and almost impossible to avoid cholesterol completely.

HOW CHOLESTEROL TRAVELS THROUGH YOUR BODY

Since cholesterol is a fat, it does not mix with water or blood, and cannot travel in the bloodstream by itself. Cholesterol and other fats (lipids), in order to travel through the bloodstream, must be wrapped in protein. The combination of cholesterol and protein is called "lipoprotein" cholesterol.

The 3 lipoproteins we will be concerned with are:

1. Very low density lipoprotein cholesterol (VLDL)
2. Low density lipoprotein cholesterol (LDL)
3. High density lipoprotein cholesterol (HDL)

Lipoproteins

Lipoproteins are classified by weight or density of the protein:

- **VLDLs** (Very Low-Density Lipoproteins) carry some cholesterol but mainly triglycerides which the liver produces from excess calories eaten. When the VLDLs travel through the blood stream, the majority of triglycerides are removed to be used as energy or stored as fat. As the process occurs, the VLDLs are gradually converted to LDLs.

- **LDLs** (Low-Density Lipoproteins) carry about 75-80% of the blood cholesterol. Cholesterol is transported by the LDLs from the liver to other parts of the body where it can be used for essential functions. LDLs appear to be responsible for depositing unused cholesterol in the artery walls leading to atherosclerosis. LDLs foster coronary heart disease and have become known as the "bad" cholesterol.

- **HDLs** (High-Density Lipoproteins) carry about 20-25% of the blood cholesterol. They transport cholesterol from the body's tissues to the liver where it is eliminated. HDLs may also carry cholesterol away from cells in the artery walls back to the liver for reprocessing or removal from the body through the bile acids. This process aids in lessening the possibility of plaque build-up, thus HDLs have become known as the "good" guys.

Why Are LDLs Called "bad" Cholesterol?

Each cell in your body has receptors which reach out to the LDLs in the blood stream and pull the LDLs into the cell for productive work in cell growth. A diet rich in cholesterol or saturated fats causes fewer receptors for LDLs to be made. If there are too few receptors for the amount of LDLs circulating in the bloodstream, some LDLs will be left in the bloodstream and return to the liver where they will be disposed of. But there will be some that will not be disposed of, and these are the ones that will become stuck on the artery walls and begin the build up of plaque. Hence the name "bad cholesterol".

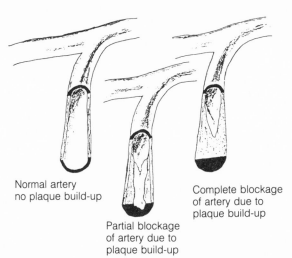

Normal artery
no plaque build-up

Partial blockage
of artery due to
plaque build-up

Complete blockage
of artery due to
plaque build-up

An obvious picture begins to emerge. Within the artery walls of a given individual who has too many LDLs floating around, plaque build up may continue until the opening of the artery becomes so narrow that the blood flow is restricted or stopped completely. Sounds like a pretty good case for calling LDLs "bad".

Increased levels of LDL cholesterol may be more closely related to increased risk of coronary heart disease than total cholesterol. Therefore a low level of LDL cholesterol, under 130, is what one should strive for. How this is achieved is discussed in the chapter, How To Lower and Control Your High Cholesterol under Monounsaturated fats.

Cholesterol Numbers

Cholesterol and triglycerides are measured in milligrams per deciliter (mg/dl) and the numbers are usually written with mgdl after the number (200 mg/dl). For easier reading, we have omitted the mg/dl and stated only the numbers.

Why Are HDLs Called "good" Cholesterol?

It is thought that the HDLs may remove excess cholesterol from the artery walls before it has a chance to build up into restrictive plaque. The HDLs carry the cholesterol back to the liver for processing or removal from the body. Therefore, HDLs have become known as the "good" guys. You should strive for a relatively high level of HDL cholesterol. How to do this is discussed under the exercise section in the chapter, How To Lower and Control Your High Cholesterol.

What Are Triglycerides and What Do They Do?

Triglycerides are fats formed in the liver when more calories are eaten than can be immediately used. They travel from the liver and intestines to the body's cells to be used for energy or are stored in fatty tissues. Triglycerides make up most animal and vegetable fats and comprise the major portion of the fat in your body.

Some research indicates that too many triglycerides in the blood stream may damage your blood vessels and increase your chance of developing atherosclerosis but the issue is still under discussion. If the theory is correct, you should strive for a low level of triglycerides. For information on how to lower your triglyceride level, see Steps 2 and 3 in the chapter How To Lower and Control Your High Cholesterol.

WHAT IS HIGH BLOOD CHOLESTEROL?

"High blood cholesterol" means that you have more cholesterol present in your bloodstream than is necessary for normal, healthy functioning. We know from studies, such as the Framingham Heart Study, that most people in the United States who suffer a heart attack have total cholesterol levels between 200 and 250.

Risk of a heart attack increases as the:

- triglyceride level rises above 150 for men and 110 for women
- the LDL cholesterol level rises above 130
- the HDL cholesterol falls below 40.

What About Ratio?

The relationship between your total cholesterol and your HDLs is one indicator of your risk for cardiovascular disease. The relationship is referred to as your ratio. The lower your ratio number, the lower your risk for cardiovascular disease. Concerning yourself with the ratio becomes more important as the total cholesterol goes higher.

To find your ratio, divide your total cholesterol number by your HDL number.

For example:

- If your total cholesterol number is 210 and your HDL number is 35, divide 210 by 35 which equals 6 and 6 is bad.
- If your total cholesterol is 210 and your HDL is 60, your ratio would be 3.5 which is very good.

Strive for a high HDL cholesterol and a low total cholesterol with a ratio of 3.5 or less.

According to various large studies, cholesterol levels below 190 along with a total cholesterol/HDL ratio below 4 seem to indicate a relatively low risk for cardiovascular disease. From all of the research we have studied, the following levels seem to have a relatively low risk of cardiovascular disease related to them.

CHOLESTEROL AND LIPID LEVEL CHART					
MEN				Triglycerides (these values are very much in debate)	
Age years	Total cholesterol	LDLs	HDLs		Cholesterol/ HDL ratio
20–59	<190	100–130	>50	<150	3.0
60 +	<210	125–140	>60	<150	3.4
WOMEN				Triglycerides (these values are very much in debate)	
Age years	Total cholesterol	LDLs	HDLs		Cholesterol/ HDL ratio
20–59	<190	100–120	>60	<100	2.5
60 +	<215	125–145	>70	<110	2.6

> = more than

< = less than

The above numbers are approximate and are not to be taken as the last word in the numbers game. After you find out your numbers and compare them with the above information, discuss them with your doctor and work together toward a lifetime of suitable numbers. These numbers are only one aspect of your cardiovascular risk; there are other factors to be considered such as: history of coronary heart disease, family history of cardiovascular problems, having diabetes, smoking, etc..

WHAT FACTORS INFLUENCE YOUR BLOOD CHOLESTEROL LEVEL?

Your blood cholesterol level is influenced by a variety of factors, some of which have more of an influence than others. Recent research has established that all of the following factors have some influence on your blood cholesterol level to one degree or another:

- Foods you eat
- Physical activity/exercise
- Weight
- Sex (gender)
- Age
- Heredity
- Stress
- Smoking
- Coffee

The foods you eat have the greatest influence on blood cholesterol levels. You can control the foods you eat. You cannot control heredity, age and gender.

Foods You Eat: The Difference Makes a Difference

Some Facts to Remember:

- Saturated fat in the diet is the number one villain in causing blood cholesterol to go higher.
- Cholesterol in foods also contributes to raising blood cholesterol but to a much lesser degree than saturated fat.
- Polyunsaturated fats will lower blood cholesterol, but they lower both the "bad" LDLs and the "good" HDLs.
- Monounsaturated fats lower only the "bad" LDLs, which is what you want. Canola and olive oils are the best sources of monounsaturated fats and should be used in place of other vegetable oils as much as possible.

Physical Activity/Exercise: A Must for Everyone

Scientific research indicates that a sedentary lifestyle may significantly lower an individual's "good" HDLs and contribute to high blood cholesterol and overweight.

Moderate and regular aerobic exercise tends to:

- Raise the "good" HDLs
- Lower triglycerides
- Burn up calories which helps reduce percentage of body fat, increase muscle mass and decrease weight, all of which are associated with lower LDLs

Weight: Something That May Need to Be Considered

Studies show that overweight individuals tend to have higher levels of total cholesterol and of the "bad" LDLs than do those of recommended weight.

Being overweight is usually the result of an intake of calories that exceeds the needs of your body. These extra calories are converted into the fat triglyceride. It is believed that triglycerides are involved in the development of atherosclerosis. So if you have never been motivated enough before to decrease the calories you eat, take heed, become motivated and increase the quality and length of your life.

Sex (Gender) and Age: It Is What It Is

Women, before menopause, usually have lower total cholesterol levels and higher "good" HDL cholesterol than do men of the same age. The higher HDLs usually give woman a lower and healthier total cholesterol/HDL ratio.

Some differences between men and women:

- After menopause, women's HDLs and total cholesterol usually increase to a higher level than men's of the same age.
- As men grow older, their HDLs usually stay about the same.
- When men lose weight, their total cholesterol/HDL ratio usually improves.
- When women lose weight, their ratio stays about the same.
- Smoking cigarettes causes a greater decline in HDL cholesterol in women than in men.

- As both men and women grow older, their "bad" LDL cholesterol tends to go up.

Heredity: May Need to Be More Conscientious in Your Efforts to Lower Your Cholesterol

You inherit from your ancestors tendencies toward certain cholesterol and blood fat levels. One extreme example is the situation where approximately 1 in 500 individuals has a genetic problem of too few LDL receptors on his/her cells causing a high LDL cholesterol. If you have a high cholesterol level which will not come down even with you doing all the "correct" things, for a long enough period of time, get checked for a genetic cause. If you have a genetic disorder contributing to a high cholesterol, then all of your blood relatives should also have their cholesterol levels checked.

Stress: Maybe Some Changes Are Needed

Stress may raise cholesterol levels, but it is possible that other factors may be the cause for the rise in blood cholesterol. For example, during periods of stress people may eat more foods that are high in saturated fat and cholesterol, which may increase their cholesterol levels rather than the stress itself. This is a chicken and egg story, which came first?

Smoking: Stop!

Cigarette smoking has a direct effect on your cholesterol level, it lowers the "good" HDL cholesterol. The more cigarettes smoked, the lower the HDLs go. If you are smoking in this day and age after all the other dialogue against smoking, what can we say except, stop! Smoking kills many while making money for others.

Coffee: Stop!

There are studies that suggest drinking coffee may upset your cholesterol components. As each day goes by, it is becoming more and more evident that coffee is detrimental to the human cells regardless of ones cholesterol level.

WHAT'S NEXT?

Now that you have a better understanding of your blood cholesterol, you should have a clearer reason for seeing the importance of taking an interest in your own personal well-being. See your physician and have your total lipid profile (cholesterol, HDLs, LDLs, triglycerides, and ratio) checked. For the method to follow, see the chapter, How To Determine If You Have High Cholesterol.

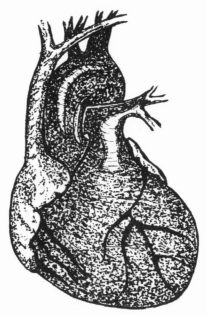

Normal Heart

2

HOW TO LOWER AND CONTROL YOUR HIGH CHOLESTEROL

This chapter explains the basic facts about lowering and/ or controlling your blood cholesterol. If you wish to learn more about the subject, just read the additional chapters, where we give information in greater detail. The more you read the more you will learn about cholesterol and your body chemistry and the more clearly you will understand how they fit together.

By closely following the correct plan and monitoring your progress with regular medical checkups, you can lower your blood cholesterol level and greatly reduce your risk of developing a cardiovascular disease. Generally, both your total cholesterol and LDL levels will begin to drop within 1 to 3 weeks after you begin your cholesterol lowering program. According to the National Cholesterol Education Program, the average person on a cholesterol lowering program will reduce his/her cholesterol level gradually, reaching the lowest achievable point over six months.

> Lower total cholesterol, lower LDLs, lower ratio and higher HDLs results in a happy heart because of a lower risk of coronary heart disease.

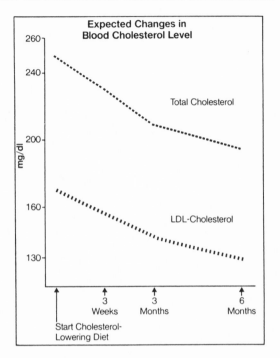

How rapidly you lower your cholesterol level and how low it goes depend on a few key factors:

- *The amount of saturated fat in your diet before beginning the program.* If you have been eating high amounts of saturated fats, you will probably see a greater reduction in your cholesterol level when you start to change your eating pattern than if your initial diet was only moderately high in saturated fat.

- *Your cholesterol level before starting the program.* In general, the higher your cholesterol level, the greater percentage of reduction you can expect.

- *How responsive your body is to your new diet.* Genetic factors play a role in determining your cholesterol level and to some extent, can determine your body's responsiveness to the cholesterol lowering program.

- *How thoroughly you follow the cholesterol lowering program.* Are you eating significantly less fat and cholesterol? Are you eating more high soluble fiber foods? Are you exercising regularly?

Because there are so many variables, such as age, gender, heredity, etc., some individuals will make more progress than others.

THREE STEPS TO LOWER YOUR CHOLESTEROL

Nothing works better than the way it is organized and managed. The easiest way to be successful in any project is to organize it in a way that allows you to follow through and manage it in the most beneficial manner. With this in mind, we have tried to present the following information in an organized way so that it can be easily understood and managed to achieve the best and quickest results. We have tried our best. The rest of the job is up to you.

Your Three Magic Steps:

1. Change the foods you eat
2. Exercise regularly
3. Reduce weight if necessary

Whether your cholesterol is high because of heredity, diet or a combination of both, your doctor will prescribe a change in the foods you eat as the first step for lowering your cholesterol. Eating correctly day by day is essential for lowering your cholesterol as many scientific studies have shown. The second most important thing you will do is regular, moderate aerobic exercise. By following these two steps, you will usually have a weight reduction as well.

STEP 1: CHANGE THE FOODS YOU EAT

The changes in the foods you eat will be subtle and appear to be small, but the difference in your body chemistry will be dramatic and significant. If you never have agreed with or understood the statement, "You become what you have eaten", understand it now as a perfect representation of how your body chemistry reflects what you have eaten. Dietary changes are very important for lowering and controlling your cholesterol level.

Three concepts you need to be concerned with:

1. Eat less fat, particularly saturated fat
2. Eat less cholesterol
3. Eat more complex carbohydrates, especially those containing soluble fiber

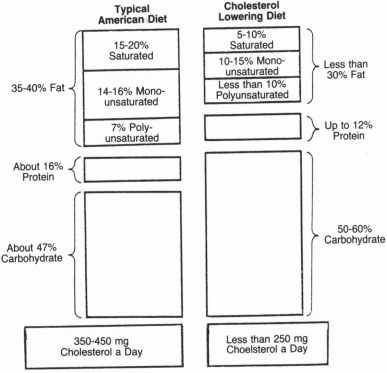

To enable you to know the specific fat, cholesterol and carbohydrate content of commonly eaten foods, we have provided a nearly complete table with the information in the back of the book.

Eat Less Fat

The typical American gets about 35% to 40% of his/her calories from fat. The American Heart Association and cholesterol experts strongly recommend that you should get no more than 20% to 30% of your calories from fat. Basic mathematics will readily show you that if you are anywhere near typical, you are eating too much fat.

Reasons for eating less fat:

- To make it easier to reduce saturated fat intake
- To promote weight reduction in overweight individuals by substituting foods with less calories

There are two major categories of dietary fat:

1. Saturated fat
2. Unsaturated fat—comprised of two types of fat:
   polyunsaturated fat   (poly-un-sat-u-rated)
   monounsaturated fat   (mono-un-sat-u-rated)

All foods containing fat are comprised of a mixture of the above fats. The combination of these fats in the foods you eat make up the total amount of fat you eat daily. Following is the recommended percentage of daily total calories you should get from each type of fat:

1. Saturated fat.................................. 5% to 10%
2. Unsaturated fat
   polyunsaturated fat........................ less than 10%
   monounsaturated fat .... 10% to 15%

Saturated Fat

The most effective way to lower your cholesterol is to eat less saturated fat. It is very important that no more than 5% to 10% of your total calories come from saturated fat because research has established; *it is saturated fat that raises blood cholesterol more than anything else you eat, even more than the cholesterol you eat.*

The major sources of saturated fats are:

- Animal products (meats, whole milk and its products)
- Three vegetable fats (coconut oil, palm and palm kernel oils, and cocoa butter)
- Hydrogenated vegetable oils

Saturated fats are solid at room temperature whereas unsaturated fats are liquid at room temperature.

Foods to Avoid in Order to Eat Less Saturated Fats

The most common foods to avoid are:

- Fat on a cut of meat
- Sausage and processed luncheon meats
- Skin of poultry
- Butter
- Whole milk cheese
- Whole milk, 2% milk and cream
- Ice cream
- Solid vegetable shortenings
- Hydrogenated vegetable oils
- Lard
- Commercially baked goods containing one or more of the following:
    Coconut oil
    Cocoa butter—found in chocolate
    Palm kernel oil
    Palm oil
- Non-dairy coffee creamers—usually contain palm or coconut oil
- Hot chocolate mixes—usually contain palm or coconut oil
- Prepared breakfast drinks—may contain palm or coconut oil

Because most fats are not able to be seen in products, you must carefully read the labels on packaged foods to determine what the fat content is. Many labels list what oils and/or shortenings are in the product, and some may list how much saturated fat there is per serving. Using this information will help you decide which foods are appropriate for you. For more label information, see Reading and Understanding Labels in the chapter, Food Logistics.

Foods to Use to Replace High Fat Foods

Try using low fat products such as:

- Lean cuts of meat: trim all visible fat—bake, roast or broil rather than fry
- Fish and white meat of poultry—have less saturated fat than red or dark meat

- Pasta, grains and legumes in place of red meat
- Tofu, a soybean product, in place of red meat
- Soft or liquid (not hard) margarine—read labels and use the one with the least amount of saturated fat and an acceptable liquid vegetable oil listed first
- Low fat cheeses—part skim mozzarella, part skim ricotta, 1% cottage, sapsago (high in sodium)
- Low fat or nonfat yogurt in place of sour cream (add chives)
- Low fat (1%) or skim milk
- Ice milk, light ice cream or sherbet—for special occasions only
- Home made baked goods made with canola or olive oil

In general, food products from land animals contain saturated fat, whereas those from water animals contain unsaturated fat.

Unsaturated Fat

Of your total caloric intake, only 20% to 25% of your calories should come from unsaturated fats. These fats are liquid at room temperature and are found primarily in vegetable oils (except cocoa butter, coconut, palm and palm kernel oils) and fish oils. Current research shows that the unsaturated omega-3 fatty acids which are found in fish have been linked with lower rates of heart attacks. It is suggested that you have fish two to three times a week in place of red meat and poultry.

Remember, there are two types of unsaturated fats:

1. Polyunsaturated
2. Monounsaturated

Polyunsaturated fats should be limited to less than 10% of your total caloric intake. They help to lower your cholesterol by lowering both the "bad" LDL cholesterol and the "good" HDL cholesterol. However, you do not want your HDLs lowered but left the same or raised. Therefore, although you do need some polyunsaturated fats in your diet, you don't want to over use them.

Polyunsaturated fats are found primarily in:

- Corn oil
- Cottonseed oil
- Safflower oil
- Sesame oil
- Soybean oil
- Sunflower oil
- walnut oil
- Wheat germ oil

Monounsaturated fats should make up approximately 15% of your total daily caloric intake. They lower only the "bad" LDL cholesterol, which is what you want, while the "good" HDLs stay about the same. This is beneficial in relation to your overall cholesterol situation.

It has been observed that in countries such as Greece, Crete and southern Italy there is a low rate of heart disease and low cholesterol levels even though the people have diets high in olive oil. In fact, studies in this country have shown that those who ate more monounsaturated fats had lower levels of "bad" LDLs than those who ate just a low fat diet.

The best sources of monounsaturated fats are:

- Avocado oil
- Canola oil, made from rapeseed
- Olive oil

When cooking and baking it is preferable to use vegetable oils high in monounsaturated fats such as canola oil (Puritan oil) and olive oil.

How to Determine the Amount of Fat You May Eat Daily

It may seem somewhat of an overkill to belabor the aspect of determining the amounts of the different types of fat permitted; we agree. In most cases you don't have to do all this nit-picking and calculating if you simply stop eating the saturated fat foods, such as butter, whole milk products, poultry skin, fatty meats and bakery goods made with palm, palm kernel and/or coconut oils. But, if you are one who requires and/or desires more information, by all means make the effort. To find the calorie and fat content of various foods, refer to the Nutritive Value of Foods table in the back of the book.

Eating less fat has two advantages:

1. You decrease your cholesterol level
2. You will more easily reach your desirable weight; if you do not need to lose weight, eat more complex carbohydrates to replace the calories lost from eating less fat.

It's important to note that fat contains more than twice the amount of calories per gram weight as protein or carbohydrate. A gram of fat has 9 calories and a gram of protein or carbohydrate has only 4 calories.

There are two steps for determining the amount of fat (hidden and visible) you may eat per day:

1. Decide how many total calories you should have per day. The chart below is an overall average of caloric intake for various ages and weights.

RECOMMENDED DAILY CALORIE ALLOWANCE				
	Age	Wt.	Ht.	Calories
Children	1-3	28 lb.	34"	1300
	4-6	44	44	1800
	7-10	66	54	2400
Males	11-14	97 lb.	63"	2800
	15-18	134	69	3000
	19-22	147	69	3000
	23-50	154	69	2700
	51 +	154	69	2400
Females	11-14	97 lb.	62"	2400
	15-18	119	65	2100
	19-22	128	65	2100
	23-50	128	65	2000
	51 +	128	65	1800

Source: Food and Nutrition Board, National Academy of Science/National Research Council

2. Once you have decided how many calories you desire or need per day from the above chart, look at the chart below to determine how many grams of fat you are permitted daily. Remember, you are to get only 20% to 30% of your daily calories from the fat you eat. If you are just beginning to lower your cholesterol, it is usually suggested you begin by lowering your fat intake to 30%. If you are unsuccessful in lowering your cholesterol to a satisfactory level, then consider decreasing your fat intake to 25% or 20% of your daily calories.

Remember, if you decrease the amount of calories you are getting from fat, you may want to replace those calories by eating more complex carbohydrates. Of course this is based on the criteria of your individual situation of whether or not you need to lose weight.

Permissible Amount of Fat To Provide 20%, 25% or 30% of Daily Calories at Specific Calorie Levels			
Calories per day	Grams of total fat that provide		
	20% of calories	25% of calories	30% of calories
	Grams	Grams	Grams
1500	33	42	50
1800	40	50	60
2000	44	56	67
2100	47	58	70
2400	53	67	80
2700	60	75	90
2800	62	78	93
3000	67	83	100

If you desire, you can determine how many grams of each type of fat you may eat daily based on the percentage of each fat allowed.

Saturated fat .... 5% to 10% of total daily calories
Polyunsaturated fat .... less than 10% of total daily calories
Monounsaturated fat............ 10% to 15% of total daily calories

Calculate your grams of each type of fat by multiplying the percentage times your total daily calories and then divide that answer by 9 (the number of calories in a gram of fat). The resulting number is the grams of that type of fat you are permitted daily.

For example: If you decide to eat a total of 1800 calories a day with 30% of the calories being fat, multiple 1800 by the percentage of each type of fat (the total percentage of the three fats should be 30%), then divide by 9.

Saturated fat = 5% of total calories (1800) = .05 x 1800 = 90 calories divided by 9 (calories per gram) = **10** grams per day.

Polyunsaturated fat = 10% of total calories = .10 x 1800 = 180 calories divided by 9 = **20** grams per day.

Monounsaturated fat = 15% of total calories = .15 x 1800 = 270 calories divided by 9 = **30** grams per day.

Thus you may eat:

Saturated fat	10 grams
Polyunsaturated fat	20 grams
Monounsaturated fat	_30_ grams
a total of	60 grams of fat daily

Most food labels will list the total amount of fat per serving. Some will also list saturated and polyunsaturated fats but usually not monounsaturated fat. To find the amount of monounsaturated, subtract the saturated and polyunsaturated from the amount of total fat. Avoid products that do not list the types and amounts of various fats. See the section Reading and Understanding Labels in the chapter on Food Logistics.

Hydrogenated and Partially Hydrogenated Oils

One last word about fats. You will see the words hydrogenated and partially hydrogenated on ingredients list. This means that unsaturated vegetable oils have undergone a process to make them more saturated or solid. These are used in various products such as vegetable shortenings, margarines and commercially baked goods to prolong their shelf life. Partially hydrogenated oils may be used in limited amounts; the hydrogenated oils should be avoided: they are the same as saturated fats.

Eat Less Cholesterol

You would think that if your cholesterol is high, the most important thing you could do to lower it would be to stop eating all foods containing cholesterol. Ironically that's not true! Eating smaller quantities of foods containing cholesterol is the key point you want to remember. Research tells us that the saturated fat you eat increases your blood cholesterol level more than the cholesterol you eat. You should however, still decrease the amount of cholesterol you usually eat.

The recommended daily intake of cholesterol is approximately 250 mg., which is a little more than the amount of cholesterol in one egg yolk. The average American eats approximately 350 to 450 mg. of cholesterol a day. Easy math suggests the average American should cut back 100 mg to 200 mg of cholesterol a day.

Cholesterol is found only in foods of animal origin:

- Meats, poultry, fish and shellfish
- Milk products
- Egg yolks

All meats and poultry contain about the same amount of cholesterol per ounce. Most fish and shellfish contain slightly less cholesterol per ounce, except shrimp which contains slightly more cholesterol than meats. Cholesterol is in the muscle and fat of these foods. Most of the cholesterol in milk is in the fat.

Cholesterol content of some common foods:

Egg yolk	210 mg
1 cup whole milk	33 mg

1 cup skim (no milk solids added)	4 mg
3 oz. regular ground beef, cooked	76 mg
3 oz. sirloin steak, lean & fat, cooked	77 mg
3 oz. liver, fried	410 mg
3 oz. sweetbreads	400 mg
3 oz. veal cutlet, broiled	109 mg
3 oz. pork chop, broiled	79 mg
3 oz. lamb chop, braised	78 mg
3 oz. chicken breast with skin, cooked	73 mg
3 oz. chicken drum stick with skin, cooked	78 mg
3 oz. flounder without added fat, cooked	55 mg
3 oz. shellfish, cooked:	
Clams	57 mg
Crab meat	
Alaskan King	45 mg
Blue crab	85 mg
Lobster	61 mg
Oysters	93 mg
Scallops	35 mg
Shrimp	166 mg
1″ cube cheddar cheese	18 mg
1 cup ice cream, vanilla (11% fat)	59 mg
1 cup frozen custard, soft serve	153 mg
1 cup sherbet (2% fat)	14 mg
1 cup frozen yogurt	13 mg
1 cup yogurt:	
made with whole milk	29 mg
made with lowfat milk	11 mg
made with nonfat milk	4 mg
1 slice cheesecake, $\frac{1}{12}$ of 9″ cake	170 mg
1 slice angelfood cake, any size	0 mg

The foods highest in cholesterol and which should be significantly limited are:

- Egg yolks
- Organ meats—liver, kidney, brain, sweetbreads, heart

For each whole egg called for in a recipe, you can usually substitute two egg whites. Avoid all organ meats, and limit your intake of meat and poultry to 4 oz. daily.

Shellfish are not high in cholesterol as is commonly thought. Shrimp has the highest level—over 150 mg. per serving. You can work shrimp into your menu once in a while without any real problem. Scallops have a low 35 mg. per serving. Compare that figure with a serving of white meat of chicken at 54 mg. What you have to relate to when eating shellfish is how it has been prepared. Has it been fried? Was butter or another highly saturated fat used in the preparation?

Read labels on packaged foods for cholesterol content per serving. However remember, when reading the listing of contents it is more important to be concerned with saturated fat than cholesterol. Beware of products whose labels state in large print on the front of the package, "NO CHOLESTEROL". They may still be high in saturated fat, which raises your blood cholesterol more severely than cholesterol itself. Look for a package whose label states "NO SATURATED FAT AND NO CHOLESTEROL."

Remember, there is no cholesterol in:	
fruits	grains
vegetables	nuts
legumes	seeds

Eat More Complex Carbohydrates, Especially Those Containing Soluble Fiber

Carbohydrates should make up 50% to 60% of your total daily calories. Carbohydrates have no cholesterol, very little saturated fat, and some unsaturated fat. They come from plants and are the chief source of energy for all body functions and muscular exertion.

There are two categories of carbohydrates:

1. Simple carbohydrates—sugars found in and derived from fruits and vegetables.
2. Complex carbohydrates—starches and fiber found in fruits, vegetables, grains, legumes, nut and seeds.

In nature, both the simple and complex carbohydrates come packaged together in fruits, vegetables, legumes, grains, nuts and seeds. Fruits have a greater concentration of simple carbohydrates than vegetables, grains and legumes which have mostly complex carbohydrates.

Fiber Can Make a Difference

Fiber, known as roughage, is a nondigestible type of complex carbohydrate which has no nutritional value but helps to keep the intestinal tract in good working condition. Fiber is very helpful in lowering high cholesterol.

There are two forms of fiber. To get the benefits of both, you need to include both in your diet. Eating a variety of fiber-containing foods daily will help you get the amount of fiber you need. Although you require 20 to 35 grams of fiber daily, most Americans eat only approximately 10 grams daily. (See chart in back of book for soluble fiber content of various foods.)

Fiber: two forms
1. Soluble—dissolves in water
2. Insoluble—does not dissolve in water

Soluble Fiber

Soluble fiber dissolves in the fluids in the intestines but is not absorbed by the body. Pectin, certain gums and psyllium are soluble fibers. One of the gums is beta-glucan, which is present in oat products and beans and appears to be very beneficial in lowering cholesterol.

Soluble fiber in the highest concentration is found in:
- Rice bran
- Oat bran
- Rolled oats
- Barley
- Legumes (dried beans and peas, lentils)
- Fruits such as apples, applesauce, apricots, boysenberries, figs, pears, dried prunes
- Vegetables such as beets, broccoli, brussel sprouts, cabbage, carrots, corn, eggplant, lima beans, peas, potatoes with skin, zucchini

Soluble fiber makes a difference and helps:

- In lowering total cholesterol by lowering the "bad" LDL cholesterol
- Slow the absorption of glucose
- Control appetite by creating feeling of fullness

That water soluble fiber aids in lowering cholesterol was first reported by Dr. James W. Anderson in 1977 at the University of Kentucky. He found that when a large amount of oat bran was eaten, the liver produced more bile acids, helping to remove cholesterol from the body through elimination. The liver also produced less cholesterol.

Since Anderson's findings, it has been established that oat bran is perhaps the most favorable source of soluble fiber for lowering your cholesterol because:

- It has a high content of soluble fiber (gum)
- It may be used in a variety of ways

Rice bran is richer in soluble fiber than oat bran; two tablespoons of rice bran have as much soluble fiber as one-half cup of oat bran. Adding two tablespoons of rice bran or one-half cup of oat bran to your diet daily will help in lowering your cholesterol. Rice bran is not as versatile in food preparation as oat bran which can be used to replace some amount of flour in baking. Rice bran can be sprinkled right from the package on top of cereals, yogurt or fruit.

Dried beans and peas are another excellent source of soluble fiber which are able to be used in a wide variety of dishes.

You can increase your soluble fiber intake by eating:

- Homemade oat and/or oat bran muffins
- Oatmeal and oat bran cereal
- Oat bran and rice bran added to other foods
- Homemade bean and lentil dishes
- More vegetables and fruits high in soluble fiber

> Dr. James Anderson recommends that if you want to lower
> your high blood cholesterol, you should eat between 6 and
> 7.5 grams of soluble fiber for every 1,000 calories you eat.
> Don't eat more than 18 grams a day though.

Insoluble Fiber

Insoluble fiber is the fiber that gives plants their stability and structure. It does not dissolve in water and is not absorbed from the digestive tract.

Insoluble fiber is found in:

- Whole grains
- Wheat and corn bran
- Legumes
- Nuts
- Most fruits
- Most vegetables
- Seeds

Insoluble fiber makes a very big difference by:

- Speeding up the time it takes for food to move through the digestive tract, it is the ultimate in natural laxatives.
- Controlling the appetite by creating a feeling of fullness.
- Preventing diseases of digestive system such as diverticulosis, constipation and hemorrhoids and possibly colon cancer.

When beginning to add fiber to your diet, do it gradually if your digestive system is not accustomed to it because you may have increased flatulence (gas). Some people may experience cramping or mild diarrhea. These problems will lessen and disappear as your digestive system adjusts to the increased fiber. Constipation should be a problem of the past; your regularity will be improved and bowel movements will be large and soft and possibly more frequent. It is important that you drink six to eight 8 oz. glasses of water daily. Your ultimate goal could be to begin your day with a bowl of oat bran cereal or oat bran muffins and end it with a delicious dried bean dish or lentil soup.

> Remember: Complex carbohydrate foods, if eaten plain, are low in saturated fat and have no cholesterol. Many have soluble fiber. Sounds like a ticket to the world of ideal foods!

It is important for you to increase the amount of complex carbohydrates you eat so that you will get the soluble fiber you need. The carbohydrates will also make up for the calories you will be losing as a result of eating less saturated fat. If you do not make up the lost calories, you may lose valuable nutrients, energy, and weight.

Foods you should eat more of to increase the complex carbohydrates in your diet:

- Dried beans and peas, lentils
- Whole grain products
- Vegetables, raw and cooked without cream sauces or gravies
- Fruits and unsweetened juices, consume more fresh whole fruit than juices

While adding more complex carbohydrates to your diet, be watchful that you do not consume more calories than your body requires to meet your needs. An excessive intake of calories, especially sugars and starches tends to elevate your triglycerides. Alcoholic beverages are very high in calories and are poor bargains for calories since they have no food value. A word to the wise is, a careful selection of foods, with moderation, and no alcohol of any kind.

These carbohydrate foods should be avoided because they are high in calories and/or saturated fat:

- Bakery products (cookies, croissants, sweet rolls, biscuits, muffins, cornbread)
- Granola cereals—usually high in fats and may have coconut
- Pastries
- Potato chips, or any chips made with fat
- Fried foods
- Refined sugars

> Calories from carbohydrates, proteins, and fats eaten in excess of immediate energy needs are converted to triglycerides. High levels of triglycerides are related to the development of atherosclerosis.

Summary and Very Brief Review of Food Changes

This very brief review is the most pertinent information you need to remember and use concerning the foods to eat when lowering your cholesterol.

- Eat less total fat, especially saturated fat, found mostly in meats, dairy products, solid shortenings, and bakery goods
- When cooking and baking:
    Do not use saturated fats—solid shortenings, lard, butter, etc.
    Decrease polyunsaturated fats—most vegetable oils
    Increase monounsaturated fats—canola and olive oils
- Eat less quantities of foods containing cholesterol, found only in animal products
- Eat more complex carbohydrates, especially soluble fiber foods—oat bran, oatmeal, rice bran, vegetables, whole grains, legumes and fruits

STEP 2: DO MODERATE AEROBIC EXERCISE REGULARLY

Step 2 is the second of the three magic steps for lowering your cholesterol. Step 1 was Change The Foods You Eat, remember? Both Step 1 and Step 2 are equal in their importance, one without the other is like putting on only one shoe. Authorities on cholesterol have well established that doing both steps is very important for reaching that balance you should be striving for in lowering your cholesterol.

Before beginning any exercise program, review your various exercise options with your doctor so you can select an activity well suited to your age and physical condition. You may need a stress test before you can determine the exercise best suited for you. Your exercise should challenge your circulatory system at an intensity that's appropriate for you.

Aerobic, endurance, exercise is physical activity which requires only a modest increase in oxygen intake. It increases your heart beat and produces beneficial changes in your respiratory and circulatory systems.

Weight lifting is not aerobic exercise and should not be done for helping to lower your cholesterol.

Exercise is most effective for the cardiovascular system if done in a rhythmic, repetitive manner which is the very nature of aerobic exercises.

Some examples of aerobic exercises are:

- Brisk walking
- Bicycling—outdoor and stationary
- Swimming
- Active dancing (aerobic as prescribed by doctor, moderate square dancing)
- Jumping rope
- Cross-country skiing
- Tennis, singles

Various studies have demonstrated that moderate aerobic exercise can:

- Increase the "good" HDLs—age has no effect on the benefit but if you smoke, you may not receive the benefit
- Decrease triglycerides
- Lower "bad" LDLs
- Reduce stress, which is associated with high cholesterol

One of the most important benefits of aerobic exercise seldom gets any notice except by the body itself. By exercising regularly, a network of small blood vessels (collateral circulation) in the heart muscle is increased and the coronary arteries open more. This allows more blood to reach the heart cells, delivering a greater supply of oxygen and nutrients. Another benefit is, if one of the coronary arteries is obstructed, the collateral circulation will still deliver blood to the area that is obstructed and less heart muscle damage will occur.

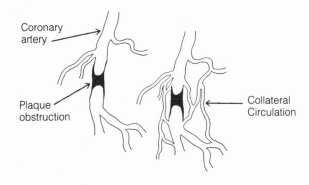

Increase of collateral circulation in coronary
artery resulting from aerobic exercise.

In order for exercise to be effective and to produce the desired results, your pulse rate must increase to a certain point. Exercise should be done for no less than 20 to 30 minutes at a time, at least three to four times a week. See the chart below for what your pulse rate should increase to during your exercise. Pulse rates at rest vary among individuals due to personal traits and physical activities. It is not uncommon among athletes to have an at rest pulse rate as low as 40 beats a minute. These athletes would not need or be able to raise their rate to those in the chart below. To be prudent, check with your doctor to find out what your pulse rate should increase to when exercising.

PULSE RATE DURING EXERCISE	
AGE	*PULSE RATE*
20	120-150 beats per minute
25	117-146 beats per minute
30	114-142 beats per minute
35	111-138 beats per minute
40	108-135 beats per minute
45	105-131 beats per minute
50	102-127 beats per minute
55	99-123 beats per minute
60	96-120 beats per minute
65	93-116 beats per minute
70	90-113 beats per minute

Source: U.S. Department of Health and Human Services

To take your pulse, place your index and middle fingers of one hand on the artery in your wrist at the base of your thumb on the other hand. Count the beats for 15 seconds and multiply times 4 to get your pulse rate (heart beat) per minute.

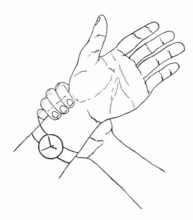

After you decide your exercise activity, it is important to:

- Know your limits, begin slowly and gradually increase the intensity and duration over the weeks.
- Always ease into (warm up) and out of (cool down) your exercise. Do five minutes of flexing and slowly running in

place at the beginning and five minutes of walking and
stretching at the end of your exercise.
- Dress appropriately and wear the proper footwear.
- Exercise only on a flexible surface, never on concrete, etc.
- Do not exercise for at least one hour after a meal.

When making the transition from inactivity to vigorous
activity, warming up with flexing exercises is important
for reducing the strain on muscles, joints and ligaments.
The warm up allows for gradual circulatory adjustment
and increases in muscle temperature, reducing the chances
of orthopedic injury and heightening muscle efficiency and
oxygen exchange between blood and tissues.

It is equally important to make a gradual transition from
vigorous activity to nonactivity. The cool down prevents
a rapid fall in blood pressure which might cause fainting,
irregular heart rhythms, or more serious complications.
Blood vessels dilate in exercising muscles. If exercise is
ended abruptly, especially if you stand motionless after
exercise, there may be a fall in your blood pressure, pool-
ing of blood in the veins and a decreased return of blood
to the heart and brain. If you cool down by walking and
stretching, your circulatory system has a chance to adjust
to your new level of activity and keep your blood moving
to all parts of your body.

So the next time you see someone going through all
those contortions before or after exercising, you now know
it's not "show biz," it's simply someone knowing and doing the correct thing.

Do not take a shower, steam bath or sauna immediately
after exercising. The external heat from these can put too
much of a burden on your circulatory system. You must
wait until your internal heat, which was increased by exercise, can be lessened and your circulation restored to
normal.

Be sure the exercise activity is one that you will enjoy
and can be done easily and year round in the area where

you live. If these factors are met, you will be much more likely to exercise frequently.

In summary, for aerobic exercise to be safe and effective, it should be:

- Suited to your needs and approved by your physician
- Done rhythmically and vigorously enough to raise the heartbeat moderately—you should breathe harder, but not to the point where you are gasping
- Sustained for at least 20 to 30 minutes and be repeated at least 3 to 4 times per week
- Preceded by a warm up and followed by a cool down period

STEP 3: REDUCE WEIGHT IF NECESSARY

Before undertaking any weight reduction program, you should get a medical evaluation. For the best overall results (lower weight and good cholesterol numbers), your weight reduction program should include both diet changes and exercise.

People who are overweight may be at higher risk for cardiovascular problems because they frequently have:

- High levels of total cholesterol
- High levels of "bad" LDL cholesterol
- High levels of triglycerides
- Low levels of the "good" HDL cholesterol

The potential benefits of weight reduction are:

- Lower total cholesterol level
- Lower LDL cholesterol level
- Lower triglycerides level
- Higher HDL cholesterol level

To achieve or maintain a recommended weight, your daily caloric intake must not exceed the number of calories your body burns daily. Therefore if you eat fewer calories and increase your physical activity on a regular basis, you should reduce your weight. It is suggested not to decrease your daily calories below what is recommended for your desired weight, for your age and height, see chart below. It is best to work with your doctor when losing weight; he may advise you to speak with a dietician or nutritionist as well.

RECOMMENDED DAILY CALORIE ALLOWANCE				
	Age	*Wt.*	*Ht.*	*Calories*
Children	1-3	28 lb.	34"	1300
	4-6	44	44	1800
	7-10	66	54	2400
Males	11-14	97 lb.	63"	2800
	15-18	134	69	3000
	19-22	147	69	3000
	23-50	154	69	2700
	51+	154	69	2400
Females	11-14	97 lb.	62"	2400
	15-18	119	65	2100
	19-22	128	65	2100
	23-50	128	65	2000
	51+	128	65	1800

Source: Food and Nutrition Board, National Academy of Science/National Research Council

A key concept to remember and use is; 3500 calories equals 1 lb of weight gain or loss. You could deplete 3500 calories a week by a combination of eating fewer calories and burning up calories through exercise. A practical approach is to target 500 calories daily (500 cal. x 7 days = 3500 cal.) by eating less and exercising more. This could lead to one pound lost per week. The slower method is the most healthy approach and has the most long lasting benefit. Weight should be reduced over a long period of time not in a short period.

ESTIMATED CALORIES BURNED BY AVERAGE 150 LB. PERSON EXERCISING 1 HOUR	
Activity	*Calories burned*
Bicycling......................	240-420
Cross-country skiing..........	600
Dancing.......................	240-420
Housework	100
Jogging, 5½ mph..............	660
Jogging, 7 mph	920
Jumping rope.................	750
Rowing	250-420
Running in place	650
Swimming, 25 yds/min	275
Swimming, 50 yds/min	500
Tennis, singles...............	420
Walking, 2 mph	240
Walking, 3 mph	320

By following the food and exercise suggestions in this chapter, you should be able to achieve your desirable weight, see following charts.

DESIRABLE WEIGHT FOR HEIGHT CHART			
*Men age 25 and over**			
height (1" heels)	*small frame*	*medium frame*	*large frame*
5' 2"	112-120	118-129	126-141
4 3	115-123	121-133	129-144
5 4	118-126	124-136	132-148
5 5	121-129	127-139	135-152
5 6	124-133	130-143	138-156
5 7	128-137	134-147	142-161
5 8	132-141	138-152	147-166
5 9	136-145	142-156	151-170
5 10	140-150	146-160	155-174
5 11	144-154	150-165	159-179
6 0	148-158	154-170	164-184
6 1	152-162	158-175	168-189
6 2	156-167	162-180	173-194
6 3	160-171	167-185	178-199
6 4	164-175	172-190	182-204

DESIRABLE WEIGHT FOR HEIGHT CHART			
*Women age 25 and over**			
height (2" heels)	*small frame*	*medium frame*	*large frame*
4' 10"	92-98	96-107	104-119
4 11	94-101	98-110	106-122
5 0	96-104	101-113	109-125
5 1	99-107	104-116	112-128
5 2	102-110	107-119	115-131
5 3	105-113	110-122	118-134
5 4	108-116	113-126	121-138
5 5	111-119	116-130	125-142
5 6	114-123	120-135	129-146
5 7	118-127	124-139	133-150
5 8	122-131	128-143	137-154
5 9	126-135	132-147	141-158
5 10	130-140	136-151	145-163
5 11	134-144	140-155	149-168
6 0	138-148	144-159	153-173

* Weight in pounds according to frame (in indoor clothing). For nude weight, deduct 5 to 7 lb. Information prepared by Metropolitan Life Insurance Company.

Calories Say, "Not All Foods Are Equal"

Plan well-balanced meals and snacks around familiar foods. Substitute complex carbohydrates for high-fat and high calorie foods. Remember, fat has nine calories per gram weight whereas carbohydrate or protein have four calories per gram weight. What better case could you have for showing, "Not all calories are equal."

To achieve or maintain a recommended weight be certain to:

- Have a sense of commitment
- Review your eating habits
- Compare how many calories you eat daily with the amount you should be eating daily
- Eat only the number of calories needed for your physical activity-for maintaining weight, not for losing weight
- Have sufficient physical activity to burn up any excess calories and/or weight

Helpful tips for reducing your weight:

- Eat three meals a day at regular times.
- Don't skip meals, it lowers your resistance to snacking between meals which may equal more calories in the end.
- Relax and sit at a table whenever you eat.
- Put your food portion on your plate and don't have seconds.
- Concentrate on enjoying your food, don't watch TV or read while you eat.
- Have raw vegetables and fruits handy for quality snacks rather than high-calorie snacks and junk food.
- Avoid fast foods, usually high in fat; instead, eat from the salad bar.
- Go grocery shopping only after you have eaten, not when you are hungry.
- Avoid all alcohol—ounce for ounce, it has almost as many calories as fat. Use mineral water with a slice of lemon or lime.
- Walk rather than ride and use stairs rather than elevator when possible.

Remember, if you are having any difficulty with either maintaining or reducing your weight, you are probably taking in too many calories in relation to your activity level. Once again you must realize that nothing works better than the way you have organized and managed it.

SUMMARY OF FOLLOWING THE THREE MAGIC STEPS	
Doing this	Results in
Eat more monounsaturated fats (canola and olive oils)	Lower LDL cholesterol level
Eat less saturated fat	Lower total cholesterol level
Eat less calories, reduce weight	Lower triglyceride level
Exercise more	Higher HDL cholesterol level
Eat less saturated fat and exercise more	Lower total cholesterol/HDL ratio

ADDITIONAL STEPS TO AID IN LOWERING YOUR CHOLESTEROL

In most cases, a cholesterol lowering diet and exercise are the only steps necessary to lower your high cholesterol.

However, there are additional things you can do that may help your cholesterol drop to even a more beneficial level.

Stop Smoking, Stop Drinking Coffee and Alcohol

In this day and age it seems absurd to have to say, "don't smoke and don't drink coffee or alcohol!." Although there are still some unanswered questions about coffee and alcohol, the show is closed when it comes to smoking. It is just a matter of time until the scientific world will bring down the curtain on coffee and alcohol as well. A health conscious person doesn't need to see act three and the curtain to come down before stopping coffee and alcohol.

Studies have shown that:

- Smoking lowers your "good" HDLs and raises your "bad" LDLs.
- Coffee may raise your blood cholesterol, triglycerides and lower your "good" HDLs.
- Alcohol in a small quantity may have some very limited benefit, but that benefit is far outweighed by all of the negative aspects of alcohol consumption. To increase your life's overall benefits, don't drink alcohol at all.

Medications for Lowering Your Cholesterol

In accordance with the National Cholesterol Education Program (NCEP), patients whose LDL cholesterol levels remain high despite adequate dietary therapy should be considered for drug treatment by their doctor. At least 6 months of intensive dietary therapy and counseling should usually be carried out before initiating drug therapy. However, if there are other risk factors (previous heart attack, smoking, high blood pressure, etc.), then possibly drug therapy should be initiated before 6 months.

For individuals with severe elevations of LDLs (>225mg/dl) or with definite coronary heart disease (CHD) for whom dietary therapy alone is unlikely to be adequate or for whom the urgency of achieving substantial cholesterol lowering is greater, it may be appropriate to consider drug therapy along with diet earlier. A minimum of three months of dietary therapy is required to establish an adequate baseline for evaluating the efficacy of subsequent drug therapy.

After an adequate trial of dietary therapy, adding medication to dietary therapy should be considered if the LDL levels are:

- Greater than 190 mg/dl (represents a very high LDL risk level): In patients without definite CHD or two other CHD risk factors (one of which can be male).
- Greater than 160 mg/dl (high risk LDL): In patients with definite CHD or two other CHD risk factors. (See Risk Factors in chapter, How Serious Is High Cholesterol?)

If medication is prescribed, you must still continue your exercise and diet, since diet always remains the cornerstone of a cholesterol lowering plan and the combination may allow you to take less medication.

If placed on medication, be certain your doctor explains:

- Exactly how and when it is to be taken (before, with or after meals)
- All the major side effects and what to do about them
- With which medical conditions the medications should not be used
- Its interactions with other medications or substances

Also be certain to have periodic monitoring of blood tests by your doctor to determine adverse reactions to the medication.

Many of the cholesterol lowering medications are potent and effective but have a potential for causing toxic effects if not monitored safely. The FDA has approved eight medications for blood cholesterol lowering. Of the eight, the National Cholesterol Education Program cited cholestyramine, colestipol and nicotinic acid (niacin, a B vitamin; do not take without medical supervision) as the medications of first choice. In its report, the National Cholesterol

Education Program emphasized the effectiveness and the long-term safety of these medications. The other medications are gemfibrozil, probucol, clofibrate and dextrothyroxine. Of this group, some are much more appropriate as treatment for some individuals then others, depending on their overall medical condition.

Inhibitors, drugs that reduce cholesterol production such as lovastatin, are very effective and new and may be a therapeutic break through. However further longterm use and experience will determine their place in therapy.

In the event you are advised to use medication, you should go to your local library and ask the reference librarian for the books titled:

- AMA Drug Evaluations
- Physician's Desk Reference (PDR)
- United States Pharmacopeia Drug Information For The Consumer

These books list medications and give you the manufactures' information including contraindications, side effects, etc. You may want to copy the pertinent details to review at your leisure. It is your personal responsibility as a patient and a consumer to know as much as possible about the substances you are taking into your body. Your doctor is your helper in maintaining your wellness, but it is your responsibility to take an interest when he/she is trying to help you. Don't just throw yourself at your physician's feet and whine; take some initiative and responsibility.

If you have a medical condition such as diabetes, gout, liver disease, peptic ulcer, etc., you must be certain your physician is aware of it before placing you on any cholesterol lowering medication. Some cholesterol lowering medications are not compatible with the above or other conditions.

CHOLESTEROL LOWERING PROGRESS CHART

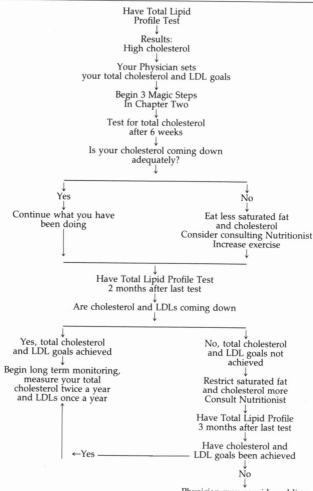

Have Total Lipid
Profile Test
↓
Results:
High cholesterol
↓
Your Physician sets
your total cholesterol and LDL goals
↓
Begin 3 Magic Steps
In Chapter Two
↓
Test for total cholesterol
after 6 weeks
↓
Is your cholesterol coming down
adequately?
↓

Yes
↓
Continue what you have
been doing

No
↓
Eat less saturated fat
and cholesterol
Consider consulting Nutritionist
Increase exercise
↓

Have Total Lipid Profile Test
2 months after last test
↓
Are cholesterol and LDLs coming down
↓

Yes, total cholesterol
and LDL goals achieved
↓
Begin long term monitoring,
measure your total
cholesterol twice a year
and LDLs once a year

No, total cholesterol
and LDL goals not
achieved
↓
Restrict saturated fat
and cholesterol more
Consult Nutritionist
↓
Have Total Lipid Profile
3 months after last test
↓
Have cholesterol and
←Yes ——————————— LDL goals been achieved
↓
No
↓
Physician may consider adding
cholesterol lowering medication

See you on the beach.

The umbrella is up; you bring the chairs.

3

3 WEEK PLAN FOR LOWERING YOUR CHOLESTEROL

Three weeks is an ideal period of time in which to make the transitions necessary for lowering your cholesterol level and becoming accustomed to the food and exercise adjustments. Some people, because of their lifestyle, personality, etc. may take a little longer to make all the necessary transitions. So do not become discouraged; each positive effort you make has a benefit toward what you are trying to achieve.

The 3 Week Plan is a structured way to follow the food and exercise information given in the previous chapter, How To Lower and Control Your High Cholesterol, and is ideal for working with your doctor and dietician/nutritionist. The Plan does not prescribe all of the foods to eat or not to eat but rather suggests foods high in soluble fiber you should be using to replace foods high in saturated fats and cholesterol.

The quantity of food to eat is usually not given; you decide the quantity based on whether or not you need to reduce your weight. It is impossible to structure a plan that is suited to everyone's needs and tastes. Subsequently the 3 Week Plan is a foundation for you to build on, according to your individual needs and tastes, by using the information in the previous chapter. As always, the information should complement your doctor's recommendations.

THE GOAL OF THE 3 WEEK PLAN

The goal of the three week plan is to give you enough information and insight so you can lower and control your cholesterol level.

To begin lowering and controlling your cholesterol level you must:

Eat less:
- Saturated fat
- Total fat
- Cholesterol

Eat more:
- Complex carbohydrates—soluble fiber
- Monounsaturated fat

Do:
- Aerobic exercise

THE METHOD OF THE 3 WEEK PLAN

When making dietary and exercise changes, it is best to make the transitions slowly so that your body can adjust properly and the changes do not overwhelm you. Sample menus are included as examples of how you can make the food transition slowly. The sample menus are only examples, they are not chiseled in stone or bone. Exercise is gradually increased by the week. These changes are made week by week.

Follow one week at a time.

1st Week—getting into position
2nd Week—moving along with additional modifications
3rd Week—locking in on lifetime eating and exercise habits

1st Week—Getting into Position

Add to shopping list:
2% milk rather than whole milk
Canola and/or olive oil rather than other vegetable oils
Oat bran
Soft margarine, with acceptable vegetable oil listed first, in place of butter
Raisins
Frozen apple juice or other flavor (used as sweetener in muffins)
Canned or dried navy, kidney, pinto and garbanzo beans
Molly McButter or Butter Buds (used in place of butter on vegetables)
Nonstick cooking spray

Don't buy:
Commercially baked goods and crackers—high in fat and usually made with palm or coconut oil
Ice cream
Prepared fried items such as chicken, fish, french fries etc.

Eat daily:
Oat bran cereal made with ⅓ cup oat bran
    or
2 oat bran muffins (preferably homemade)
    or
½ cup cooked beans (navy, kidney or pinto)

8 glasses of fluids—4 to 6 of water & 2 to 4 of other fluids

Do:
Use 2% milk
Eat no more than 2 egg yolks per week
Use canola and/or olive oil in place of other vegetable oils
Use soft margarine rather than butter
Not eat fried foods
Decide what aerobic exercise you plan to do and discuss with your doctor if it is appropriate for you
Begin aerobic exercise slowly

1st week sample menus

Breakfast:
orange juice, ½ to 1 cup

oat bran cereal, made with ⅓ cup oat bran
2% milk, ½ to 1 cup
whole grain toast, 1 or 2 slices
soft margarine, 1 to 2 tsp.
water, eight ounces

Snack: (optional)
V-8 juice, ½ to 1 cup

Lunch:
lean roast beef sandwich
tomato, lettuce & cucumber salad
apple
water, eight ounces

Snack: (optional)
whole grain English muffin
soft margarine, 2 tsp.

Dinner:
chicken breast, baked
corn
cauliflower, sprinkled with grated parmesan cheese
asparagus with molly butter
whole grain roll
soft margarine, 1 tsp.
fresh fruit cup
tea, 1 cup

Breakfast:
grapefruit juice, ½ to 1 cup
soft boiled egg
whole grain toast, 1 to 2 slices
soft margarine, 1 to 2 tsp.
2% milk, 1 glass

Snack: (optional)
banana
water, 1 glass

Lunch:
water, 1 glass
oat bran muffins, 2
soft margarine, 2 tsp.
low fat cottage cheese, ½ cup
crushed pineapple, 3 Tbs. mixed into cottage cheese

carrot sticks
tea, 1 cup

Snack: (optional)
    toasted whole grain bagel, 1
    soft margarine, 1 tsp.

Dinner:
    lean sirloin steak, 4 oz.
    baked potato with Butter Buds
    carrots with ginger
    green beans
    whole grain roll
    soft margarine, 1 tsp.
    angel food cake topped with fresh unsweetened fruit

Breakfast:
    grapefruit, ½
    french toast
    soft margarine, 2 tsp.
    fruit only preserves
    2% milk, 1 glass

Snack: (optional)
    Rye Krisp crackers, 5
    2% milk, 1 glass

Lunch:
    tomato juice, 1 glass
    tuna fish pita sandwich
    raw broccoli & cauliflower flowerets
    apple

Snack: (optional)
    dried apricots, 4 or 5

Dinner:
    navy bean soup
    salad
    whole grain bread
    margarine 2 tsp.
    tea, 1 cup

2nd Week—Moving Along With Additional Modifications
Add to shopping list:
    1% milk rather than 2% milk
    Lean cuts of red meat—not prime or choice cuts

Very lean ground beef
Poultry
Lentils
Pasta
Low fat cheeses
Lots of fruits and vegetables high in soluble fiber
    prunes, apples, dried apricots, pears, figs, dates, citrus, broccoli, brussel sprouts, carrots, corn, lima beans
Sugar-free preserves

Don't buy:
Continue with recommendations for 1st week
Lunch meats
Frozen vegetables with sauces or butter
Whole milk products

Eat daily:
Continue with 8 glasses of fluids
1 serving of fruit containing soluble fiber

Oat bran cereal & 2 oat bran muffins
    or
Oat bran cereal & ½ cup cooked beans
    or
2 oat bran muffins & ½ cup cooked beans
    or
1 cup cooked beans (chili, baked beans, bean soup)
    or
4 oat bran muffins

Do:
Continue with recommendations of 1st week
Trim all visible fat from meat before and after cooking
Remove skin from poultry before cooking
Use 2 egg whites in place of each egg called for in recipes
Use 1 % milk
Eat only low fat dairy products—cheese, yogurt
Use evaporated skim milk in place of cream or half & half
Aerobic exercise 3 to 5 days for 20 to 30 minutes

2nd week sample menus

Breakfast:
  stewed prunes
  oat bran pancakes made with 1% milk and egg whites
  margarine, 2 tsp.
  unsweetened applesauce or jam
  1% milk, ½ to 1 cup

Snack: (optional)
Kavali cracker with 2 tsp. peanut butter (natural, no hydrogenated
    oil)

Lunch:
  ham (3½ oz) sandwich on whole grain bread
      with lettuce and tomato
  tart apple
  tea

Snack: (optional)
  oat bran muffin
  1% milk

Dinner:
  oven fried chicken, skin removed
  corn
  spinach
  boiled potatoes with parsley
  margarine, 1 tsp.
  oat bran muffin
  margarine, 1 tsp.
  fresh strawberries

Breakfast:
  orange cut in eighths
  oat bran muffins, 2
  margarine, 2 tsp.
  1% milk, 1 glass

Snack: (optional)
  peach

Lunch:
  lentil soup
  vegetable salad

whole grain toast
margarine, 2 tsp.

Snack: (optional)
strawberry milkshake

Dinner:
turkey stroganoff
noodles
green beans
carrots
seedless grapes

Breakfast:
cantaloupe
oat bran cereal
1% milk, ½ to 1 cup

Snack: (optional)
lowfat plain yogurt with fresh fruit added (strawberries, banana,
peach)

Lunch:
chili
whole grain bread
margarine, 2 tsp.
gelatin

Snack:
Rye-Krisp cracker and low fat cheese

Dinner:
spaghetti with lean ground beef meat sauce
grated parmesan cheese, 3 Tbs.
vegetable salad
whole grain French bread
baked apple

3rd Week—Locking in on Lifetime Eating and Exercise Habits

Add to shopping list:
Nonfat or skim milk rather than 1% milk
Tofu—soybean product
Fish and/or seafood
Light Miracle Whip Salad Dressing rather than mayonnaise
Nonstick cooking spray

Lean ground turkey
Turkey or chicken cutlets
Barley
Rice bran
Cornmeal

Don't buy:
Continue with recommendations for 1st and 2nd weeks
Prepared soups—usually high in fat and salt

Eat daily:
Continue with recommendations for 1st & 2nd weeks
2 servings of fruit containing soluble fiber
At least 1 serving of vegetable containing soluble fiber

Do:
Continue with recommendations for 1st & 2nd weeks
Eat fish or seafood
Eat lean ground turkey rather than ground beef
Eat 2 meatless meals
Use light Miracle Whip and mustard on sandwiches
Use light dressings on salads
Use only sugarless jam or jelly rather than margarine on breads
    and muffins
Aerobic exercise 3 to 5 days for at least 30 to 40 minutes

Snacks:
Air-popped popcorn
Pretzels
Fresh or dried fruit
Raw vegetables

3rd week sample menus

Breakfast:
banana breakfast drink, made with skim milk
corn muffin, 2
unsweetened jelly

Snack: (optional)
dried apricots

Lunch:
lentil soup
salad

whole grain bread or toast with unsweetened jam
low fat frozen yogurt

Snack: (optional)
raw vegetables
toasted plain corn tortilla

Dinner:
shrimp Creole
brown rice
cheesy zucchini
spinach salad
seasonal fruit cup

Breakfast:
fresh pineapple
oat bran pancakes
unsweetened applesauce
skim milk, 1 glass

Snack: (optional)
figs or dates

Lunch:
lowfat cottage cheese with fresh fruit
whole grain muffin, 2
celery & carrot sticks
tea

Snack: (optional)
air-popped popcorn

Dinner:
broiled salmon
rice
margarine, 2 tsp.
snow peas, steamed
beets
oatmeal muffins, 2
unsweetened applesauce

Breakfast:
orange cut in eighths
oatmeal with 2 Tbs. raisins
skim milk, $\frac{1}{2}$ to 1 cup

Snack: (optional)
  lowfat plain yogurt with applesauce and cinnamon added

Lunch:
  minestrone soup
  oat bran muffins, 2
  tea

Snack: (optional)
  pear

Dinner:
  lean ground turkey meatloaf
  baked potato
  brussel sprouts
  lima beans

For the rest of your life follow the 3rd week of the plan with the following modifications.

Eat:

  Fish 2 to 3 times a week
  A meatless meal (tofu, pasta, beans, lentils) at least 2
    to 3 times a week
  No more than 2 egg yolks per week
  Poultry 3 to 4 times a week
  Very lean red meat no more than 2 or 3 times a week
  Foods high in soluble fiber daily

Do:

  Aerobic exercise for at least 30 to 40 minutes 3 to 5
    days per week

DAILY FOOD REVIEW AND ACCOUNTING

Some individuals involved in the game plan of lowering their cholesterol find it useful to do a daily food intake review and accounting chart. If you are one of these individuals, we have supplied a blank chart (chart #3) at the end of this chapter that can be copied and used to list the foods you have eaten that day. You can then do an accounting of the total calories, fat, and cholesterol you have eaten for the day to see if you are within the recommended limits.

Also supplied are a model chart for a "present" or "before" eating style and a model chart showing a "cholesterol lowering" or "after" eating style. If you compare the totals of these two charts, you will easily notice the differences in the fat, cholesterol, soluble fiber and calorie intake. Be sure to also note that in the cholesterol lowering chart, the foods are not dull or small in quantity.

You may want to complete a chart for the way you are presently eating and another for after you begin the cholesterol lowering plan. After completing your charts, compare your total intake in the various columns with the recommendations given in the chapter, How To Lower And Control Your High Cholesterol. This is a dramatic way of seeing how the types of foods and the way they are prepared can change the amount of calories, fat, cholesterol and soluble fiber you eat.

Complete your charts by using the Nutritive Value of Foods and the Soluble Fiber Content of Various Foods tables in the back of the book.

A review of chart #1:

- 51% of the calories are from fat (169.3 gms. × 9 calories/gram divided by 2962 calories). This is much more than the recommended total daily fat intake of 20% to 30% of total daily calories.
    - Saturated fat is 20% of the total calories, should be below 10%.
    - Polyunsaturated fat is 10%, the highest acceptable level.
    - Monounsaturated fat is 18%, higher than the recommended level of 10% to 15%.
- 554 mg. of cholesterol is very high compared to the recommended level of 250 mg daily.
- 8.9 grams of soluble fiber is below what some authorities suggest should be a daily intake of 12 to 18 grams.

DAILY FOOD DIARY—PRESENT EATING STYLE

Food Eaten	Amount	Calories	Total Fat	Satu-rated Fat	Poly-unsatu-rated Fat	Mono-unsatu-rated Fat	Choles-terol	Soluble Fiber
Chart #1			Grams	Grams	Grams	Grams	Milli-grams	Grams
Fried egg	1	95	7	2.7	0.8	2.7	278	0
bacon	3 slices	110	9	3.3	1.1	4.5	16	0
wheat toast	2 slices	140	2	0.8	0.6	0.8	0	0.6
butter	1 Tbs	100	11	7.1	0.4	3.3	31	0
orange juice	1 cup	110	tr	tr	tr	tr	0	0.2
bologna	3 slices	270	24	9.2	2.1	11.4	46	0
Amer. cheese	2 slices	105	9	5.6	0.3	2.5	27	0
wheat bread	2 slices	140	2	0.8	0.6	0.8	0	0.6
mayon-naise	1 Tbs	100	11	1.7	5.8	3.2	8	0
potato chips	20 ch	210	14	3.6	7.2	2.4	0	0.1
coke	12 oz	160	0	0	0	0	0	0
pork chop	3 oz	330	26	9.6	3.0	12.1	88	0
Baked potato	1	220	tr	0.1	0.1	tr	0	2.0
butter	1 Tbs	100	11	7.1	0.4	3.3	31	0
sour cream	3 Tbs	75	9	4.8	0.3	2.1	15	0
cooked carrots	½ cup	35	tr	tr	tr	tr	0	1.0
cooked peas	½ cup	62	tr	tr	0.1	tr	0	2.0
butter	1 tsp	33	3.5	2.4	0.1	1.1	10	0
vegetable salad	2 cup	32	tr	tr	0.3	tr	0	0.4
French dressing	2 Tbs	130	12.8	3.0	6.8	2.4	4	0
apple pie	1 slice	405	18.0	4.6	4.4	7.4	0	2.0
Totals	xxx	2962	169.3	66.4	34.4	60.0	554	8.9

Now as a comparison, look at the delicious food and the quantities on chart #2 and compare the totals of the two charts (chart #1 and chart #2).

As you can see from chart #2:

- 24% of the calories are from fat (55.5 gms × 9 calories/gram divided by 2105 calories), within the recommended total fat intake of 20% to 30% of total daily calories. The 24% shows a limited fat intake and yet plenty of food was eaten.
  - Saturated fat is 6% of total calories, within the acceptable amount.
  - Polyunsaturated fat is 6.45%, within the acceptable amount.
  - Monounsaturated fat is 9%, good amount but could be slightly more if desired.
- 108.25 mg. of cholesterol is well below the 250 mg limit.
- 13.4 grams of soluble fiber is right on target.

For more detailed information on the amount of fat to eat, see the section in chapter Two, How To Determine the Amount of Fat to Eat Daily.

Stay on course.
Fill out your charts
and use them to set your sail.

DAILY FOOD DIARY—FOR CHOLESTEROL LOWERING

Food Eaten	Amount	Calories	Total Fat	Satu-rated Fat	Poly-unsatu-rated Fat	Mono-unsatu-rated Fat	Choles-terol	Soluble Fiber
Chart #2								
		Grams	Grams	Grams	Grams	Grams	Milli-grams	Grams
orange	1	60	tr	tr	tr	tr	0	0.3
oatmeal	1 cup	145	2.0	0.4	1.0	0.8	0	2.0
1% milk	½ cup	80	1.5	0.75	tr	0.4	3.5	0
wheat toast	1 slice	70	1.0	0.4	0.3	0.4	0	0.3
marga-rine	1 tsp	33	3.5	0.6	1.6	1.3	0	0
apple	1	125	1.0	0.1	0.2	tr	0	1.5
bean soup	2 cups	340	12.0	3.0	3.6	4.4	2.0	2.5
lettuce	1 bowl	20	tr	tr	0.2	tr	0	0.2
low/cal dressing	1 Tbs	25	2.0	0.2	0.9	0.4	2.0	0
orange gelatin	1 cup	140	0	0	0	0	0	0
oat bran muffin	1	100	3.5	0.5	1.0	1.9	0	2.0
marga-rine	1 tsp	33	3.5	0.6	1.6	1.3	0	0
peanuts	1 oz	165	14.0	1.9	4.4	6.9	0	0
roasted chicken	3 oz	140	3.0	0.9	0.7	1.1	73.0	0
baked potato	1	220	tr	0.1	0.1	tr	0	2.0
low fat plain yo-gurt with chives	2 Tbs	24	0.5	0.3	tr	0.1	1.75	0
broccoli	1 cup	45	tr	0.1	0.2	tr	0	2.0
cauli-flower	½ cup	15	tr	tr	tr	tr	0	0.5
parme-san cheese	2 Tbs	50	4.0	2.0	tr	0.8	8.0	0
sherbet	1 cup	270	4.0	2.4	0.1	1.1	14.0	0
Totals	xxx	2105	55.5	14.25	15.9	20.9	108.25	13.4

YOUR DAILY FOOD DIARY

Chart #3			Total Fat	Satu-rated Fat	Poly-unsatu-rated Fat	Mono-unsatu-rated Fat	Choles-terol	Soluble Fiber
Food Eaten	Amount	Calories						
		Grams	Grams	Grams	Grams	Grams	Milli-grams	Grams
Totals	xxx							

4

FOOD LOGISTICS

As you have discovered from the reading, the food you eat is your first line of defense and attack against high cholesterol. To enable you to be in an greater degree of control, you will need to make some minor changes or modifications in the foods you eat.

There are four areas of concern:

1. Planning   determine the foods that are best for helping you lower your cholesterol level

2. **Shopping**   use a list of needed foods to help you avoid the foods detrimental to your progress

3. **Preparation**   use cooking methods best suited to lowering your cholesterol level

4. **Eating out**   take your time ordering and ask questions about how food is prepared

Major changes in your body chemistry and your overall well-being can be brought about by small changes in your eating habits and lifestyle. The changes in eating habits begin with what you buy and bring home from the grocery store and what you eat when dining out.

PLANNING: WHAT FOODS TO EAT

Review your overall eating pattern and see where you need to make changes to lower or control your cholesterol. Do you need to stop eating fatty foods such as lunch meats, hot dogs, hamburgers and other meats and begin eating more nonmeat meals with beans, lentils or pasta?

In planning what foods you should be eating, ask yourself:

- What is the fat content?
    What type of fats (you want low saturated fat content)?
    What percentage of the calories per serving come from fat?
- What is the cholesterol content?
- How many calories per serving?
- Does it have any water soluble fiber?
- Is it a complex carbohydrate rather than a simple carbohydrate?

If you eat few foods high in saturated fat, an occasional high saturated fat food won't raise your blood cholesterol level. If you anticipate a high saturated fat, high cholesterol day, eat an especially low saturated fat, low cholesterol diet the day before and the day after. For example, if you are planning to attend a picnic or reception, sandwich that day between two days of highly modified eating.

Remember, your goal is to limit the saturated fat and cholesterol in your diet each day. You don't need to cut out all the high saturated fat and high cholesterol foods. But try to substitute one or two low saturated fat or low cholesterol foods each day; soon you will reach your goal of a low saturated fat, low cholesterol diet. This is called behavior modification and should be done in a peaceful and controlled fashion. All behavior modification is best reinforced with objective (without prejudice or emotions) thought and information.

The number and size of servings should be adjusted to reach and maintain your desirable weight. Use the chart below to be sure you are eating an adequate amount from each food category daily.

RECOMMENDED DAILY FOOD PLANNING GUIDE

Food Category	Nutrients	Number of Servings

Dairy products
1 serving
   1 cup milk/yogurt
   1½ oz. cheese
   ½ cup cottage
      cheese
	Protein
	Fat
	Carbohydrates
		2 for adults
		3 for teenagers
		3 when pregnant or
		   breastfeeding

Eggs 1 serving 2 eggs	Protein Fat	3 yolks/week Unlimited whites

Meats, poultry,
fish
1 serving
   2 oz. cooked
Meat the size &
thickness of woman's
palm = 3 to 5 oz.,
man's = 5 to 7 oz.
	Protein
	Fat
		1 to 2
		No more than 4 oz.
		   3 to 5 days/week

Beans
1 serving
   1 cup cooked
      dried peas,
      beans, lentils
   2 Tbs. natural
      peanut butter
	Protein
	Carbohydrates
	Fat, very little
		Use in place of
		   meat, poultry,
		   fish

Fats and oils	Fat	No more than 6 to 8 teaspoons a day

Fruits
1 serving
   ½ cup juice
   ½ cup cooked
   1 cup raw
   1 medium fresh
   ½ grapefruit
   wedge of melon
   ½ cup berries
   ¼ cup dried
	Carbohydrates	2 to 4

Vegetables
1 serving
   ½ cup juice
   ½ cup cooked
   1 cup raw
	Carbohydrates	3 to 5

continued on next page

Food Category	Nutrients	Number of Servings

Grain products
1 serving
  1 slice bread
  ½ bun or
    English muffin
  1 small roll,
    biscuit or
    muffin
  4-6 crackers
  ½ cup cooked
    cereal, rice or
    pasta
  1 oz. ready to eat
    cereal
	Carbohydrates
	Protein
	Fat, a little
		6 to 11

SHOPPING FOR FOODS

The supermarket is the perfect place to begin making the changes in what you will be eating. Choose a wide variety of foods that are:

- Low fat
- Low-cholesterol
- High soluble fiber

Some basic suggestions for shopping are:

- Never go grocery shopping when you are hungry or near mealtime. This is usually when your willpower is at its lowest and impulse buying is at its highest.
- Have a shopping list which has only high soluble fiber, low fat and low cholesterol items listed. Buy only those items.
- Head for the produce section first, stocking up on fresh fruits and vegetables.
- Choose low-fat meat, poultry, fish, low-fat dairy products, dried beans and peas, whole grain products, and vegetable oils high in monounsaturated fats.
- Buy mostly from the outside aisles. Commercially prepared foods and many "impulse" items are placed on the inner aisles and are often the sources of hidden fats, especially saturated fat.
- Read and compare food labels for fat, fiber and cholesterol content.

If you stock your kitchen shelves with foods that are low in saturated fat and cholesterol, it will be much easier to adjust your eating habits. With a little additional thought, time and effort in the beginning, you can learn to shop for these foods quickly. Treat yourself with kindness by making these minor adjustments.

Reading and Understanding Food Labels

Nutrition information on packaged food products helps you select foods suitable to your dietary requirements. Nutrition labels identify the types and amounts of nutrients provided in the packaged food. Reading labels will help you find foods that are low in fat, especially saturated fat, and cholesterol.

When shopping, compare labels. You want to buy foods with low total fat and no or low saturated fat and cholesterol. All food labels list the product's ingredients in order by weight. The ingredient in the greatest amount by weight is listed first. The ingredient in the least amount by weight is listed last.

To avoid too much total or saturated fat, limit your use of products that list a fat or oil first or that list many fat and oil ingredients. The list below identifies the names of common saturated fat and cholesterol sources in foods.

SOURCES OF SATURATED FAT AND CHOLESTEROL		
Animal fat	Egg and egg yolk solids	Palm kernel oil
Bacon fat	Ham fat	Palm oil
Beef fat	Hardened fat or oil	Pork fat
Butter	Hydrogenated	Turkey fat
Chicken fat	vegetable oil	Vegetable oil*
Cocoa butter	Lamb fat	Vegetable
Coconut	Lard	shortening
Coconut oil	Meat fat	Whole-milk
Cream		solids

* Could be coconut or palm oil

Check the types of fat on the ingredient list of the package and ask yourself some questions, such as:

- Is it an animal fat, coconut oil, palm oil, palm kernel oil or hydrogenated vegetable oil? All are high in saturated fat and are the oils you want to **avoid**.
- Is it corn, cottonseed, safflower, sunflower or soybean oil? All are high in polyunsaturated fat and may be **used in moderate amounts**.
- Is it avocado, canola (rapeseed), olive oil? All are high in monounsaturated fat and are the oils you **want to use most often**.

Some labels show the amount of total fat in grams per serving. The label may also list the:

- Percentage of calories from fat
- Amount of polyunsaturated fat
- Amount of saturated fats
- Amount of cholesterol

The amount of monounsaturated fat is seldom listed, but you can approximate it by doing two steps of basic math:

1. Add the polyunsaturated and saturated fats
2. Subtract them from the total fat content for the amount of monounsaturated fat

---

With the information on the label, you can compare the fat and cholesterol content of different products. Choose products with a low proportion of saturated fat and a high proportion of monounsaturated fat.

The following charts show how to identify products with lower saturated fat and cholesterol. These charts help you understand product labels more easily. Labels give the amount of fat in grams (g) and cholesterol in milligrams (mg) per serving.

Take note, 2% milk and skim milk have less fat and cholesterol than whole milk. Tub margarine has less saturated fat and cholesterol than stick butter.

Nutrition Information Per Serving	Whole milk	2% milk	Skim milk
Serving size	1 cup	1 cup	1 cup
Calories........................	150	121	86
Protein	8 g	8 g	8 g
Carbohydrates..................	11 g	12 g	12 g
Total fat	8 g	5 g	< 1 g
Polyunsaturated..............	< 1 g	< 1 g	0 g
Saturated.....................	5 g	3 g	< 1 g
Cholesterol	33 mg	18 mg	4 mg
< means less than			

Nutrition Information Per Serving	Butter, stick	Margarine, tub
Serving size	1 Tb	1 Tb
Calories.............................	101	101
Protein	0.1 g	0.1 g
Carbohydrates.......................	0.1 g	0.1 g
Fat (100% calories from fat)...........	11.4 g	11.4 g
Polyunsaturated...................	0.4 g	3.9 g
Saturated.........................	7.1 g	1.8 g
Cholesterol	31 mg	0 mg

Note: The amount of monounsaturated fat is not listed for either product.

When comparing nutrition information, be sure you are comparing the same serving size with each item, for example, Tbs. with Tbs., cup with cup, lb. with lb. etc. Notice that some brands of margarine information are in tsp. and other brands are in Tbs.

Following a low-saturated fat, low-cholesterol diet is a balancing act. It requires eating the variety of foods necessary to supply the nutrients your body needs without eating:

- Too much saturated fat
- Too much cholesterol
- Too many calories.

One way to assure variety, and at the same time a well-balanced diet, is to select foods each day from each of the following food groups. Also select different foods from within groups, especially foods low in saturated fat (second column). Portions and the size of each portion should be adjusted to reach and maintain your desirable weight. As a guide, the recommended daily number of portions is listed for each food group.

MAKING THE RIGHT CHOICE			
Food Groups	Choose	Go Easy On	Decrease

Meat (2 to 3 servings per week, total 6 oz.)	lean cuts of meat with fat trimmed, such as:
	 • beef
	  round, sirloin, chuck, loin
	 • lamb
	  leg, arm, loin rib
	 • pork
	  tenderloin, leg (fresh), shoulder (arm, picnic)
	 • veal
	  all trimmed cuts except ground
			"Prime, Choice" Fatty cuts of meat, such as:
			 • beef
			  corned beef brisket,
			  regular ground short ribs
			 • pork
			  spareribs, blade roll fresh frankfurters sausage, bacon luncheon meats organ meats

Poultry, Fish, & Shellfish (up to 4 oz./day)	poultry without skin fish shellfish canned fish packed in water		goose, domestic duck self-basting turkey caviar, roe
Dairy Products (2 servings/day; 3 servings for teens or when pregnant or breastfeeding)	skim milk, 1% milk, low-fat buttermilk, low-fat evaporated or nonfat milk low-fat or nonfat yogurt low-fat soft cheeses like cottage, pot, farmer, sapsago cheeses labeled 2 to 6 grams fat/oz.	2% milk yogurt part-skim ricotta part-skim or imitation hard cheeses "light" cream cheese "light" sour cream	whole milk & its products; cream, half & half, non-dairy creamers, imitation milk products, whipped cream custard style yogurt neufchatel brie, swiss, American, mozzarella, feta, cheddar, muenster cream cheese sour cream
Eggs (3 yolks/week)	egg whites		egg yolks

Food Groups	Choose	Go Easy On	Decrease
Fats & Oils (up to 6 to 8 tsp./day)	unsaturated vegetable oils: olive, canola, peanut, safflower, corn, sesame, sunflower, soybean margarine made with unsaturated oils, liquid or tub	nuts seeds avocados olives	butter, coconut oil, palm oil, palm kernel oil, lard, bacon fat margarine or shortening made with saturated fat
Breads, Cereals, Pasta, Rice, Dried Peas and Beans	whole grain bread, English muffins, dinner rolls, pita, rice cakes low-fat crackers; matzo, bread sticks, kavli, rye krisp, saltines, zwieback, soda crackers, pretzels hot cereals, most cold dry cereals pasta; plain noodles, spaghetti, macaroni any grain rice dried peas & beans, split peas, black-eyed peas, chick peas, kidney beans, navy beans, lentils, soybeans, tofu	store-bought pancakes, waffles, biscuits, muffins, cornbread	croissant, butter rolls, sweet rolls, Danish pastry, doughnuts most snack crackers; cheese crackers butter crackers those made with saturated oils granola-type cereals made saturated oils pasta & rice prepared with cream, butter or cheese sauce; egg noodles
Fruits and Vegetables (2 to 4 servings fruit, 3 to 5 servings vegetables/day)	fresh, frozen (plain), canned or dried fruits and vegetables		vegetables prepared in butter, cream or sauce
Sweets and Snacks (avoid too many sweets)	low-fat frozen desserts; sherbet, sorbet, Italian ice, frozen yogurt, popsicles low-fat cakes; angel food cake low-fat cookies; fig bars, gingersnaps low-fat snacks; plain pop-corn, nonfat beverages; carbonated drinks, unsweetened juices, tea	ice milk, homemade cakes, cookies & pies using saturated oils sparingly fruit crisps & cobblers	high-fat frozen desserts, ice cream, frozen tofu high-fat cakes; most store-bought cakes, pound & frosted cakes store-bought; pies, most cookies, candy, high-fat snacks; chips, buttered popcorn high-fat beverages; frappes, milkshakes, floats, eggnog

PREPARATION OF FOODS

When you prepare foods at home, you have a great opportunity to control:

- Selection of foods
- Ingredients
- How foods are prepared

You will lower your cholesterol level greatly by making minor changes in the foods you select and how you prepare them.

An aspect of cooking to lower and control your cholesterol is **using** vegetable oils low in saturated fat and high in monounsaturated fat and **avoiding** oils and fats high in saturated fat. Below is a guide to help you select the more favorable oils to use.

CHECK YOUR COOKING FATS AND OILS			
Oil	Fat %	Characteristics	Cooking Uses
Almond	Sat. 7% Mono. 64% Poly. 29%	Strong, toasted nutty flavor; low smoke point, not good for deep frying	Salad dressings, chicken salad; small amount in nutty baked items
Avocado	Sat. 7% Mono. 71% Poly. 21%	Rich; high smoke point	Great in salads; appropriate for fast and deep frying and sauteing
Bacon fat	Sat. 39% Mono. 49% Poly. 12%	Low smoke point	Frying
Butter	Sat. 66% Mono. 30% Poly. 4%	Low smoke point	Used in baking
Canola (Rapeseed)	Sat. 6% Mono. 60% Poly. 33%	Light, clear, bland; high smoke point; all purpose	Very good for baking; blends well for salad dressings
Chicken fat	Sat. 31% Mono. 47% Poly. 22%		Frying

Oil	Fat %		Characteristics	Cooking Uses
Coconut	Sat.	90%		Used in many commercially baked goods
	Mono.	6%		
	Poly.	2%		
Corn	Sat.	13%	Good, "corny" taste; general purposes	Good for baking, great for pie crust and making popcorn
	Mono.	24%		
	Poly.	59%		
Lard	Sat.	41%	Not much flavor	Used in baking and frying
	Mono.	47%		
	Poly.	12%		
Margarine	Fats not broken down because individual margarines vary greatly and there is no "average" margarine. When selecting a margarine choose one with an acceptable liquid vegetable oil listed first on the ingredient list and with the lowest level of saturated fat.			
Olive	Sat.	14%	**Extra Virgin:** Fruity, robust flavor; deep greenish-gold; medium smoke point	Perfect in salads, stews, sauces & cheese dishes; good for light sauteing
	Mono.	77%		
	Poly.	8%		
			Classico: Subtle, traditional flavor; medium-high smoke point	For meat, poultry, vegetables, sauces & salads; perfect for pan-frying
			Extra Light: Very slight mild flavor and light bouquet; light gold color	Suitable for all kinds of cooking, from sauteing
			high smoke point	delicate fish to baking cakes & muffins; ideal for shallow & deep frying
Palm	Sat.	50%		Used in many commercially baked items
	Mono.	38%		
	Poly.	10%		
Palm Kernel	Sat	85%		Used mostly in commercially baked items
	Mono.	12%		
	Poly.	2%		
Peanut	Sat.	17%	Slightly heavy, nutty flavor; can "flash" at high temperatures	Perfect for stir-fries; good for salads
	Mono.	46%		
	Poly.	32%		

continued on next page

Oil	Fat %		Characteristics	Cooking Uses
Safflower	Sat. Mono. Poly.	9% 12% 75%	Bland; general use	All types of cooking; use to dilute strong flavored oils; blends well
Sesame	Sat. Mono. Poly.	14% 40% 42%	Made from untoasted seeds is light & bland flavor; from toasted seeds is rich with strong flavor	Untoasted for stir-fries, salads & pan frying Toasted in small quantities for salad dressings and Oriental dishes
Solid vegetable shortening	Sat. Mono. Poly.	32% 53% 15%	High smoke point	Used in baking and deep frying
Soy	Sat. Mono. Poly.	14% 23% 58%	Prominent taste if unrefined; high smoke point	General use
Sunflower	Sat. Mono. Poly.	10% 20% 66%	Almost tasteless and odorless; all purpose	Good for salads, stir-fries, frying & sauteing; blends well; may be used to dilute stronger oils
Walnut	Sat. Mono. Poly.	9% 23% 63%	Rich, slightly nutty; low smoke point	Excellent for salad dressing; sauteing on low heat; toss with pasta or in potato or chicken salad

Note: The fat composition of the above oils can vary depending on the source.

LINING UP THE PREFERABLE OILS

Saturated Fat		Monounsaturated Fat	
Canola	6%	Olive	77%
Almond	7%	Avocado	71%
Avocado	7%	Almond	64%
Safflower	9%	Canola	60%
Sunflower	10%	Peanut	46%
Corn	13%	Sesame	40%
Olive	14%	Corn	24%

A quick glance at LINING UP THE PREFERABLE OILS reveals that:

- Both Almond and Avocado oils have the best combination for being low in saturated fat and high in monounsaturated. Unfortunately these oils are not general purpose oils and are not readily available.
- Canola oil is the next best choice. It is the lowest in saturated fat and high in monounsaturated fat, is an all purpose oil, and is readily available in stores.
- Olive oil is the highest in monounsaturated fat but has more saturated fat than the other three. Olive oil is a good choice, is versatile, and readily available.

In case you have not noticed from the chart, CHECK YOUR COOKING FATS AND OILS, be sure to take a look at the saturated fat content of:

- Coconut oil
- Palm oil
- Palm kernel oil

This should give you a clear idea why certain commercial foods must be avoided. Read labels!

> **Put bottles of various types of vegetable oils in your freezer overnight. In the morning those low in saturated fat will pour freely, but those higher in saturated fat will be less pourable. Try it and see!**

Low Fat Cooking Tips

Vegetables
- Steam, boil or bake; saute or stir-fry in small amount of broth or water instead of oil or butter.
- Season with herbs, spices, lime or lemon juice rather than with sauces, butter or margarine.
- Use lemon juice or vinegar with water and herbs for salad dressing.
- When sauteing meats, drain all excess fat before continuing with cooking.
- Bake poultry stuffing separately rather than inside poultry.

Meat, fish and poultry
- Remove skin from poultry before cooking.
- Trim fat from meat before and after cooking.
- Roast, bake, broil, or simmer.
- Cook on rack so fat will drain off.
- Baste with fat-free ingredients such as wine, tomato juice or lemon juice instead of fatty drippings. If you feel you must baste with a fat, use a monounsaturated vegetable oil.
- Use nonstick pan for cooking so that added fat will not be necessary.
- Heat slowly so that meat will brown in its own juices, eliminating the need for butter or oil.
- Chill broths and soups until fat becomes solid on top, easily removed and disposed of.

Baked goods
- Try whole grain flours to enhance flavors when using fewer fat and cholesterol-containing ingredients.
- Try using oat bran and rolled oats for baked items.
- Use monounsatured oils in place of melted or solid shortenings, butter and margarine.
- Use high monounsaturated margarine in place of solid butter or shortening.
- Use low-fat, nonfat milk or fruit juice when whole milk called for in recipe.
- Use 2 egg whites in place of each whole egg called for.

Miscellaneous
- Prepare soups, stews and gravies ahead of time and refrigerate till able to skim fat off top. To hurry the process, place in freezer for short time or place large jar of ice cubes in soup, stew or gravy. Or use large fat skimmer to pour off fat and avoid the cooling process.
- Limit egg yolks to one per serving when making egg dishes and use additional egg whites for bulking out the serving.
- Use nonstick spray made from vegetable oil or use nonstick pans that require no greasing. If you have neither, put a couple drops of vegetable oil in pan, spread it around and then lightly wipe out with paper towel.
- Eat a least one or two meatless meals per week, including bean soup, pasta, or lentils.
- Eat fish or seafood two to three times per week.

Low-fat dessert ideas:
- Fresh fruit
- Angel food cake
- Sherbet
- Gelatin
- Ice milk
- Frozen low fat yogurt

Low-fat snacks
- Air popped popcorn seasoned with spices—onion, garlic, etc
- Plain nonfat yogurt with chopped fresh fruit added
- Raw vegetables—carrots, snow peas, cauliflower, broccoli, green beans
- Fresh fruit
- Toasted shredded wheat squares sprinkled with small amount of grated parmesan cheese
- Toasted whole grain English muffin or whole grain bread with small amount nonsugar jelly
- toasted plain corn tortillas
- rye krisp, soda crackers, melba toast
- beverages—water, skim milk, fruit or vegetable juice, mineral water with a twist of lemon or lime

---

Handy broth cubes—freeze in ice cube trays left over defatted meat or vegetable broth. Remove from tray when frozen and store cubes in container in freezer. Cubes are ideal to be used as seasonings or for sauteing in place of butter or oil.

SUBSTITUTIONS

Instead of	Use
Sour cream	Plain low-fat yogurt or blended or whipped low-fat cottage cheese
Mayonnaise	Mustard for sandwiches or Yogurt mixed with mustard, lemon juice, herbs and spices
Cream	Evaporated skim milk
Whole milk	1%, nonfat or skim milk
1 Tbs. butter	1 Tbs. soft margarine or ¾ Tbs. vegetable oil
Butter on vegetables	Sprinkle on Butter Buds or Molly McButter
Pouring melted fat over	Use pastry brush to put on fat—much less used
Greasing pans with shortening	Vegetable cooking spray use nonstick pans
Whole milk cheese	1% cottage cheese, low-fat American cheese, farmer/pot cheese, partskim mozzarella, combine parmesan and sapsago for spaghetti
Solid shortenings	Soft margarine with acceptable liquid oil listed first
Melted butter or margarine	Olive or canola oil
Ground beef	Low-fat ground veal or turkey
Barbecued ribs	Chicken barbecued without skin
Meats	Tofu
Lunch meats	Sliced turkey, chicken or lean roast beef, water packed tuna fish

Instead of	Use
Commercial soups may be high in fat	Homemade bean, split pea, vegetable or minestrone soup
Chocolate	3 Tbs. cocoa plus 1 Tbs. monounsaturated oil for each square (1oz.) of chocolate
Peanut butter with hydrogenated oil	Natural peanut butter with no hydrogenated oil; store jar upside down

EATING OUT

Eating out has become a national pastime. Foods in restaurants can be a prime source of hidden fats. Too often an individual on a cholesterol lowering diet overreacts to the need of being careful when eating out. The classic comment is, "I won't be able to go out to eat anymore." Nothing could be further from the truth. However, you will have to follow some definite guidelines. Since adjustment is the height of personal intelligence, be intelligent, make the adjustment.

Eating anywhere (restaurants, friends' homes, picnics, hospital, air and train travel) other than at home does require some additional effort on your part. But it doesn't have to be a traumatic event, and you shouldn't become a recluse just because you need to be watchful of what you eat. By keeping a few facts in mind you can enjoy eating out no matter what the setting.

Some ideas to help you when eating out:

- Choose the restaurant carefully by calling the restaurant in advance and asking the following questions:
  - Is there a salad bar?
  - How are the meat, chicken and fish dishes prepared?

- Are there low-fat and high fiber selections on the menu?
- Can you have menu items broiled or baked without added fat instead of fried?

The more frequently you eat out, the more important these issues can become. Seafood restaurants usually offer broiled, baked or poached fish, and you can often request butter and sauces on the side so you can control the amount you eat. Many steak houses offer small steaks and have salad bars.

- Try ethnic cuisines. Italian and Asian restaurants often feature low fat dishes. You must be selective and alert to portion size. Try a small serving of pasta or fish in a tomato sauce at an Italian restaurant. Many Chinese, Japanese, and Thai dishes include plenty of steamed vegetables and a high proportion of vegetables to meat. Steamed rice, steamed noodle dishes and vegetarian dishes are good choices too. Some Latin American restaurants feature a variety of fish and chicken dishes low in fat.

- Make sure you get what you want; don't be intimidated by the atmosphere, menu, waiter, friends, or anything else. Here are just a few things you can do to make sure you are in control of the situation when you eat out:

  - Ask how various foods are prepared.
  - Select clear rather than cream soups.
  - Do not hesitate to request that one food be substituted for another.
  - Order appetizers low in cholesterol and/or saturated fat such as seafood cocktail or fruit or vegetable juice.
  - For main course order pasta with steamed vegetables or tomato sauce.
  - Select a green salad or baked potato in place of french fries.
  - Request sauces and salad dressings on the side and use only a small amount.
  - Ask that butter not be sent to the table with your rolls or ask for soft margarine.

- Request fruit, sherbet or angel food cake for dessert instead of baked goods or frozen desserts which are usually made with ingredients high in saturated fat and cholesterol.
- If you're not very hungry, order two low fat appetizers rather than an entire meal, split a menu item with a friend, get a doggie bag to take half of your meal home, or order a half-size portion.
- When you have finished eating, have the waiter clear the dishes away so that you can avoid postmeal nibbling.

- Learn and look for terms on the menu that denote low fat preparation or saturated fat and cholesterol preparation.

  - Terms usually associated with low fat and low cholesterol preparation:
    Steamed
    In its own juice
    Broiled
    Roasted
    Poached
    Dry broiled
  - Terms usually associated with saturated fat and cholesterol preparation:
    Buttery, buttered, in butter sauce
    Sauteed, fried, panfried, crispy, braised
    Creamed, in cream sauce, in its own gravy, hollandaise
    Au gratin, parmesan, in cheese sauce, escalloped
    Marinated, stewed, basted
    Casserole, prime, hash, pot pie

If Invited

If you casually let your friends know that you are on a low cholesterol, low fat diet, then they will know how to adjust when they invite you to dinner. If foods are served that are on your no-no list, just take a very small portion and go heavy on the permitted foods. Don't make a big ado and say you aren't allowed to eat something that was served. Remember the principle, the height of intelligence is adjustment.

If you are asked what foods you do not eat, mention such foods as red meat and fried foods. Most people can adjust their menu planning around your food needs if they are interested.

Don't make eating the center of your life. Eat to live, don't live to eat. Socializing should be the important event rather than the food and drink. Don't be conspicuous or make an issue about what you do or do not eat. Your friends, relatives and everyone else simply do not want to hear it, so keep it to yourself, it's your body chemistry you are taking care of.

Also be aware of pressure to eat foods you shouldn't. Just say, "No thank you," and don't make any explanation. If you do have to take it, just don't eat it. Become a smart politician, stay in control of the situation.

How can you tell if there is an elephant hiding in your refrigerator? Check the butter for footprints.

Heather Flint

5

HOW SERIOUS IS HIGH CHOLESTEROL?

There are important reasons for you to be concerned about the level of your cholesterol. High cholesterol increases the risk of atherosclerosis (ath-er-o-scle-ro-sis) which increases the risk of disorders of the cardiovascular (circulatory) system. The cardiovascular system consists of the heart and all of the body's blood vessels (arteries, veins, and capillaries).

Atherosclerosis contributes directly to:

- Heart Disease (Coronary Heart Disease)
- Stroke
- Other circulatory problems

In plain terms, high cholesterol can → atherosclerosis → stroke, heart attack and/or other circulatory problems.

Your future and your overall well-being are directly related to how seriously you concern yourself with your own health care. You, yourself, are the only one who can do what is necessary to prevent cardiovascular disease. Don't take the risk of cardiovascular disease lightly; make certain that you and your doctor understand each other and work together for your well-being.

ATHEROSCLEROSIS

Atherosclerosis (ath-er-o-scle-ro-sis) comes from the Greek word *athero*, meaning gruel or paste, and *sclerosis*, meaning hardness. Deposits of fatty substances, cholesterol, cellular waste, calcium and fibrin (clotting component in blood) build up in the inner lining of an artery. This build-up is called plaque. A partial or total blockage of blood flow through the artery may occur where there is plaque build- up. Atherosclerosis contributes directly to heart disease and stroke.

Arteriosclerosis (ar-te-ri-o-scle-ro-sis) is a general term for the thickening and hardening of the arteries. Arteries are the blood vessels (tubes) carrying blood, which contains oxygen and nutrients, from the heart to the cells throughout the body. Normal healthy arteries have smooth muscular walls that propel the blood along toward the various body organs.

When the inner wall of an artery has rough plaque build-up, the artery narrows, the flow of blood slows, and a blood clot (thrombus) is more likely to form than in a healthy artery. The clot forms because blood is designed to clot when it comes in contact with foreign substances and reacts to the plaque as a foreign substance.

Plaque build-up is a slow, progressive process that may begin even as early as childhood. In some people, the build up progresses rapidly in their thirties while in others it begins in their fifties or sixties. Most researchers into atherosclerosis believe this process begins because something damages the innermost layer of the artery and, over a period of time, substances from the bloodstream enter the artery wall. These substances gradually build up (plaque) and eventually narrow and block the artery.

> **The predominant fatty substance found in atherosclerotic plaque, is cholesterol.**

There are three potential causes of damage to the walls of your arteries:

1. Elevated levels of cholesterol and triglycerides
2. High blood pressure
3. Cigarette smoking

Plaque may build up at various areas within your body but the most common areas appear to be:

- The carotid arteries, located in the neck and carry blood to the brain
- The coronary arteries, located in the heart muscle and carry blood to the heart itself
- The renal arteries leading to the kidneys
- The femoral arteries in the legs

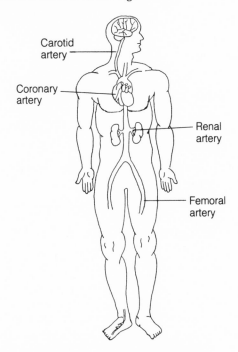

Heart Disease (Coronary Heart Disease)

The human heart is a muscle which pumps blood throughout the body. The heart has its own blood vessels, the coronary arteries, which carry blood to nourish the heart and keep it alive.

If the coronary arteries become clogged with fatty substances and cholesterol, the arteries may become so narrow or completely blocked that the heart muscle no longer receives the quantity of blood and oxygen it needs. Chest pain (angina pectoris) may result. This may be the first symptom of heart disease. But some people never have angina and experience their first symptom in a heart attack which may be fatal.

The primary cause of heart attacks is atherosclerosis, also known as coronary artery disease.

There can be two results of coronary artery disease:

1. Heart muscle damage may result from a decreased flow of blood to an area of the heart because of partial blockage of the coronary arteries to that specific area.
2. Heart attack (myocardial infarction) results from a complete blockage of the blood flow to an area of the heart muscle (myocardium). That part of the heart muscle may actually die because it is deprived of the oxygen and nutrients its cells need. Depending on how much of the heart muscle is damaged, disability or death can result.

Regular exercise increases the collateral circulation in the heart muscle and helps deliver more blood to the heart muscle.

Risk Factors for Coronary Heart Disease

The Framingham Study has shown that cholesterol levels above 160 are directly related to coronary heart disease. The higher the cholesterol level, the greater the risk for coronary heart disease.

Besides high cholesterol, the following factors place an individual at high risk for having a heart attack.

One of the following:

- Previous heart attack
- Angina

OR

Two of the following:

- Male gender
- Family history of premature CHD (parent, sibling having myocardial infarction or sudden death before age 55)
- Smoking
- High blood pressure
- HDL cholesterol under 35
- Diabetes mellitus
- Impaired circulation to the brain and/or legs
- Overweight

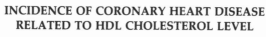

INCIDENCE OF CORONARY HEART DISEASE RELATED TO HDL CHOLESTEROL LEVEL

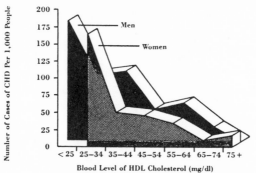

This chart from the Framingham Heart Study relates the incidence of coronary heart disease (per 1,000 men and women) to the HDL cholesterol level

The close relationship of cholesterol to heart disease has been unequivocally demonstrated by the Lipid Research Clinic Coronary Primary Prevention Trials involving 3,806 men with significantly elevated cholesterol. This study established that for every 1% decrease in blood cholesterol level, heart attacks and sudden deaths decreased by 2%.

Heart attacks are the number one cause of death in America. Statistics from the America Heart Association indicate that approximately 1,500,000 people suffer from a heart attack annually, and more than 500,000 of them will die.

Even though heart attacks are the number one cause of death in America, you can greatly help protect yourself and your loved ones by slight changes in:

- What you eat
- Your lifestyle

Stroke

Stroke is one form of cardiovascular disease. It is an injury to the nervous system which occurs when an adequate supply of oxygen and nutrients is prevented from reaching portions of the brain. The inadequate supply of oxygen and nutrients is often the result of an obstruction of the flow of blood in or to the brain. Causes of obstruction are a clot or a build-up of plaque in an artery leading to or in the brain.

Most often a clot forms in the artery at the site of the blockage. But sometimes a clot breaks off from an artery somewhere else in the body and travels through the larger blood vessels until it becomes wedged in a smaller cerebral (brain) artery. Brain cells quickly deteriorate and die when they are deprived of the oxygen rich blood normally supplied by the artery.

When the cells die, that area of the brain no longer functions. Subsequently, the part of the body controlled by this area of the brain can't function, causing unconsciousness, paralysis of part of the body, and impairment of speech, vision, thought and memory patterns. All of these effects may range from mild to severe, and from treatable to permanent. The severity of the problem depends on the extent and location of brain cell damage and the ability of the body to compensate and restore a blood supply to injured areas of the brain.

A stroke is usually the culmination of a progressive disease that may extend over many years and is not always detectable in a routine physical examination. Since in many cases there are no warning signs, a stroke is a particularly terrifying event. According to the American Heart Association, approximately 500,000 Americans suffer strokes each year and about 70-80% of the strokes are caused by blood clots in an artery. These strokes may not be fatal but are a major cause of disability.

About 2,000,000 stroke victims are alive today in the United States. Your number one protection against having a stroke is the food and behavior modification plan presented in this book! Please start using the information immediately!

Other Circulatory Problems

Just as the arteries supplying blood to the brain and heart may have atherosclerosis so can the arteries supplying other areas of the body. For example this can occur in the renal arteries leading to the kidneys and the femoral arteries leading to the lower part of the legs. If blockage occurs in the femoral artery, a condition known as arteriosclerosis obliterans may occur. This condition is most common in men over the age of 50 who :

- Smoke
- Have high cholesterol
- May also have diabetes

Depending on where the artery in the leg is blocked, the location of the pain resulting from the blockage can range from the hip to the foot. Ulcers on the foot, toes and/or heel may develop due to the lack of sufficient oxygen and nutrients being supplied to the area. The most severe result would be gangrene of the affected area and possible amputation of the affected limb.

If you haven't understood it before, understand it now: a change in lifestyle (stop smoking; exercise more, etc.) and the foods you eat are of primary importance for avoidance of circulatory problems.

Can Atherosclerosis Be Reversed?

According to Dr. Julian M. Whitaker, Director of the National Diabetes and Heart Institute in Huntington Beach, California, atherosclerosis can be reversed. Various studies have shown, that in a percentage of people who follow a cholesterol lowering program over a period of time, significant progress can be made in reversing the condition.

Studies have shown that in individuals whose cholesterol level has fallen:

- Plaque build-up will **stabilize** in some individuals
- Plaque build-up will **recede** in some individuals
- Plaque build-up will **progress** in some individuals

As a condition, atherosclerosis is a degenerative process active below the skin level of your body, out of sight and too often out of mind. It is an insidious process requiring a long period of time to create the damage caused by plaque build-up which lessens the flow of blood or causes an actual blockage.

The best policy to adopt, when dealing with a degenerative condition affecting your general health, is avoiding the circumstances and substances which lead to the degenerative condition. However, in cases where atherosclerosis already exists, try to alter those things which contribute to the condition.

Research indicates that in some individuals there is an actual reversal of plaque build-up after they have followed a low cholesterol, low saturated fat, and high monounsaturated fat food program and have done regular, moderate aerobic exercise for an extended period of time. And that is what this handbook is all about, so please, please, please use the information provided and try to spare yourself and your loved ones unnecessary agony.

6

HOW TO DETERMINE IF YOU HAVE HIGH CHOLESTEROL

Most often with your health, you are concerned with how well you feel and look, and you leave it at that. However, with the concern of cholesterol, it is not a matter of how well you feel or look but how well your cardiovascular system (heart and blood vessels) is functioning. Unlike most health conditions, there are no telltale symptoms to warn you if your cholesterol is high.

The cardiovascular conditions that high cholesterol can lead to cause symptoms only after the damage has been done. Therefore, it is your responsibility to find out what your cholesterol level is before you have any cardiovascular symptoms and hopefully avoid ever having any problems. Sounds like a pure and simple case for preventive medicine.

In choosing a physician, be certain he/she can communicate easily and knowledgeably about the condition, and does not just use a few "buzz words." You should feel comfortable asking questions and feel that the questions are answered with a true interest, concern and knowledge. In some respects, choosing the right physician to help you is the most important thing you can do.

GET THE TEST: THE TOTAL LIPID PROFILE

Generally speaking, experts in the cholesterol field recommend that cholesterol levels should start being checked in the early teenage years. If the results are normal, then about every five years thereafter. The National Cholesterol Education Program Expert Panel's Report recommends that every adult age twenty and over be tested every five years.

If there is a family history of high cholesterol and/or coronary heart disease (under 50 years of age in males and under 60 for females), then a child should be tested soon after the age of two. If the results are within the normal range, the test should be repeated every two to three years. Children with total cholesterol over 170 could possibly benefit from dietary counseling and increased exercise. Be certain to keep a running record of the test results so you can see if there is any great change occurring over the years.

Take special note; there are two different tests for determining your cholesterol level:

1. TOTAL CHOLESTEROL TEST

2. TOTAL LIPID PROFILE (Lipoprotein Analysis) which includes the following 5 components:
   1) Total cholesterol
   2) LDL cholesterol
   3) HDL cholesterol
   4) Triglycerides
   5) Total cholesterol/HDL cholesterol ratio

For your first test, probably only the total cholesterol will be ordered. We feel this is not the better way to go because it's possible for your total cholesterol to be within the "desirable" range, but for one of the components (LDLs, HDLs, triglycerides, or the total cholesterol/HDL ratio) to be too high or low. If you or your doctor were not aware of these high or low values, then you would not be treated according to your real needs and your risk of having a medical problem would not be resolved. You would have a false sense of security because you wouldn't know all of the information necessary for a complete picture. Get the complete picture by getting complete information. This can only be accomplished by having the complete test. Get the TOTAL LIPID PROFILE TEST!

The best procedure for determining your cholesterol level:

- Ask your doctor to order a total lipid profile test (total cholesterol, HDLs, LDLs, triglycerides and total cholesterol/ HDL cholesterol ratio).

- Fast twelve to fourteen hours before the test to permit a more accurate test of the triglyceride level which rises appreciably after eating. Avoid alcohol for 24 hours before the test. In general, the most favorable time to have the test is between 7 and 9 am after having not eaten from 7 pm the night before. Only water is permitted during this time.

- Sit for at least 5 minutes before your blood is drawn. Sit (do not lie down or stand) when your blood is being drawn. The tourniquet should be used for as brief a time as possible, less than a minute.

It is most important that you get this test immediately!

NOTE:
- Do not have the test taken:
  - Just after you have been seriously ill
  - Within three months of a heart attack
  - During the last trimester of pregnancy
  - After a major weight loss
  - After sudden dietary changes

  These situations interfere with a true cholesterol reading.

- Since there have been labs which have not performed the test according to professional standards, call the lab where you plan to have the blood sample taken and ask if:
  - It is accredited by a national agency, such as the College of American Pathology.
  - Its equipment is check daily.
  - Its testing results are audited regularly by an independent agency.

  You want to have the test performed in a lab that answers yes to both questions. You may ask to see their certificate of accreditation.

- Always have your test performed at the same lab.

CHOLESTEROL NUMBERS GAME, UNDERSTANDING IT

Blood cholesterol is measured in milligrams per deciliter; a deciliter is approximately one-tenth of a quart. If your cholesterol is 189 mg/dl, this means that the cholesterol found in a deciliter of liquid weighs 189 milligrams. For comparison, 28,350 milligrams equals only 1 ounce.

In order to determine whether you have high cholesterol, the values (numbers) of **all** of your blood lipids (cholesterol, HDLs, LDLs, triglycerides) and total cholesterol/HDLs cholesterol ratio need to be known. These values are used to indicate your risk of developing cardiovascular disease. A few days after you have had your cholesterol test, your doctor will receive the test results and should give you specific information as to what these numbers mean. It is most important that you do not content yourself with a general statement that the test was " normal" or "okay"; get the specific numbers. Ask questions and talk it out with your doctor. Your doctor is your foremost health adviser and is the best source for the scientific information required to understand your body chemistry.

Ask for a copy of the test results for your records; compare them with the charts below and keep them in a safe place so they can be compared with your other tests over the years.

CLASSIFICATION OF CHOLESTEROL LEVELS FOR ADULTS			
	Desirable Level	Border-line High Level	High Level
Total Cholesterol	<200	200-239	>240
LDL Cholesterol	<130	130-160	>160
< lower than > higher than			

National Heart, Lung, and Blood Institute

Formal scientific information about desirable and un-desirable levels of cholesterol in children is extremely lim-ited. The Lipid Research Clinics Program suggests the fol-lowing:

SUGGESTED CHOLESTEROL LEVELS FOR BETWEEN 2 AND 19 YEARS OF AGE			
	Normal Level	Moderately High Level	High Level
Total Cholesterol	<170	170-185	>185
LDL Cholesterol	<110	110-125	>125
< lower than > higher than			

The Lipid Research Clinics Program

RATIO IN RELATION TO RISK OF CORONARY ARTERY DISEASE			
	Low risk	Average risk	High risk
Cholesterol/ HDL ratio	3.3	4.5	6.0

Harvard Medical School Health Letter 3/5/89

The above charts do not give you any values for tri-glycerides and HDLs. There remains some controversy over the relationship between triglycerides and coronary heart disease. Some studies seem to show a definite re-lationship while other studies do not. According to Dr. Kenneth Cooper, in his book, "Controlling Cholesterol," generally, triglycerides should be less than 100 to 120 for men and even lower for women. Anyone with a level between 250 and 500 has approximately twice the risk of cardiovascular disease as someone with a lower level.

Concerning your HDL level, the ratio of your HDLs to your total cholesterol is more important than the HDL level itself. According to the findings of the Framingham Study, the average HDL level of American men is 45 and for

American women, 55. This means men and women are at average risk when their HDLs are at these levels. But again the HDL level only has real meaning when it is compared to total cholesterol. Therefore, the higher your HDL level the better because a high HDL level leads to a lower ratio which is what you want for being at a low risk for cardiovascular disease.

What the Specific Numbers Mean

Most of the research that has been done about cholesterol relates to the relationship between cholesterol levels and the risk for coronary heart disease. To date there has not been as great an effort on the relationship between cholesterol and stoke or other circulatory problems.

Various studies show that your risk for coronary heart disease may increase greatly if you have one or more of the following:

- Total cholesterol level above 200
- HDL cholesterol level below 45 for men and 55 for women
- LDL cholesterol level above 130
- Triglyceride level above 150
- Total cholesterol/HDL cholesterol ratio above 4.5

An expert panel of the National Heart, Lung, and Blood Institute believes that the level of LDL cholesterol is more closely associated with coronary risk than is total cholesterol.

VISUAL AIDS TO HELP YOU TRACK YOUR CHOLESTEROL LOWERING PROGRESS

It is a good idea to keep a running record of your cholesterol test results so you can see the progress you are making. Enter in the chart below your test results as soon as you receive them so you will have the benefit of a running record.

PERSONAL CHOLESTEROL RECORD				
	Initial test	6 Week test	3½ Mos. test	6½ Mos. test
Cholesterol				
LDLs				
HDLs				
Chol/HDL Ratio				
Triglycerides				

Using your test result numbers, you can make right angle graphs to plot your progress of lowering your Total Cholesterol, LDLs, Triglycerides, Ratio and raising your HDLs. The graphs enable you to visualize your progress. We have shown a model graph with a blank one along side for your own personal use.

SAMPLE GRAPHS

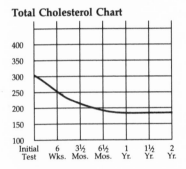

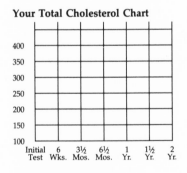

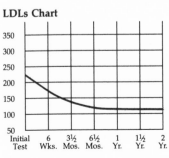

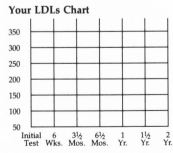

HDLs Chart

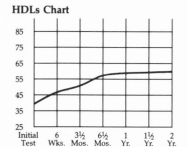

Your HDLs Chart

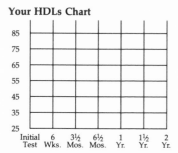

Ratio Chart

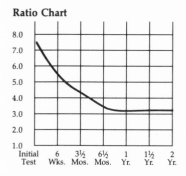

Your Ratio Chart

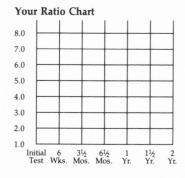

Triglyceride Chart

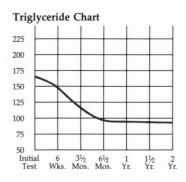

Your Triglyceride Chart

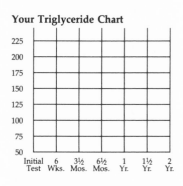

7

QUESTIONS
AND
ANSWERS

Q. How does the body get cholesterol?
A. Two ways:

1. Body makes the little it needs
2. Foods of animal origin that we eat

Q. Why should I be concerned about my cholesterol level?
A. Over time, cholesterol, fat and other substances can build up in the walls of your arteries (atherosclerosis) and slow or block the flow of blood to your organs, particularly to your brain, heart, kidneys and lower extremities. This can lead to heart attack, stroke or other cardiovascular conditions. Therefore, the cholesterol level in the circulating blood should be properly regulated.

Q. What are the statistics concerning Americans that give rise to the alarm of cholesterol in relation to cardiovascular disease?
A. The facts are that each year:

- 1½ million Americans suffer heart attacks
- ½ million suffer strokes

Almost one in two Americans will eventually die from cardiovascular disease. Medical research has established that a high blood cholesterol level is a significant contributor to cardiovascular disease.

Q. What is atherosclerosis?
A. It is a slowly developing process in which the lining of the arteries

becomes coated with fatty substances such as cholesterol. These deposits result in scarring and narrowing of the arteries which eventually may close off completely, either because the deposits have grown to together or because a blood clot has caught on the deposits (plaque).

Q. What can be the result of decreased blood flow or blockage of blood flow to organs?
A. a) If in or to your heart, you may have a heart attack
    b) If in or to your brain, you may have a stroke
    c) If in a lower extremity, you may have leg or foot pain, leg or foot ulcers which could even result in gangrene

Q. At what age should a person be concerned about cholesterol?
A. Although the problems resulting from high cholesterol do not usually show up until the adult years, the accumulation of fatty substances may begin in childhood. Therefore, forming correct eating and exercising habits in childhood may prevent a high cholesterol later. It is suggested that everyone 20 years of age and older be tested for high cholesterol. If there is a family history of high cholesterol or cardiovascular disease then young children, after the age of two, should be tested.

Q. What is the first thing I should do if I am concerned about my cholesterol?
A. The first thing you should do is to stop eating foods that contain saturated fat. The next things to do are:

- Read the chapter How To Determine if You Have High Cholesterol
- Ask your doctor to order a total lipid profile blood test
- Read the chapter How to Lower and Control Your High Cholesterol

Q. Is there more than one test for determining my blood cholesterol level?
A. Yes, there are two separate tests:

1. The total cholesterol test
2. The total lipid profile test.

We believe it is important to get the total lipid profile rather than just the total cholesterol. For more information, see the chapter, How To Determine If You Have High Cholesterol.

Q. What will lowering my cholesterol level do?

A. Lowering your high cholesterol will slow, possibly stop, and perhaps reverse fatty buildup in the walls of the arteries. The process will reduce your risk for cardiovascular problems and may save your life too!!

Q. Is there evidence that lowering my cholesterol will help me?

A. Most assuredly yes. The scientific information has been well established that lowering your cholesterol will help ward off cardiovascular disease. It is generally accepted that lowering your cholesterol 1% reduces your risk for heart disease by 2%.

Q. What factors influence my cholesterol level?

A. • Diet
    • Weight
    • Physical activity/exercise
    • Genetics
    • Gender
    • Age
    • Smoking
    • Stress

For a more detailed explanation, see the chapter, Understanding Cholesterol

Q. What is more important to eat less of, saturated fat or cholesterol?

A. Saturated fat that you eat causes blood cholesterol to rise more than the cholesterol you eat. Therefore, it seems to be more important to eat less saturated fat than cholesterol even though you should also decrease the amount of cholesterol you eat.

Q. How do I know what foods are high in saturated fats?

A. Animal products as a group are the major source of saturated fat plus coconut oil, palm kernel oil, palm oil and cocoa butter which are found in many commercially baked goods. See the food content chart in the back of the book for specific fat content of various foods, and read food labels for ingredients when buying products.

Q. Since olive oil is good for you, may I use it in unlimited quantities?

A. First and foremost, olive oil is a fat and should be used sparingly. However, olive oil is known to be low in saturated fat and high in monounsaturated fat and is therefore healthier than corn, safflower, soybean and other polyunsaturated oils.

Q. What are the most concentrated sources of saturated fat?

A.   • Coconut oil, palm kernel and palm oil are the most concentrated
           source of saturated fat, They are from 50 to 90% saturated
         • Butter is 66% saturated
         • Lard is 41% saturated

Q. Which foods listed are highest in cholesterol?

         • Peach pie
         • Crab meat
         • Cashews
         • Avocados
         • Coconut oil

A. Of the five foods listed, only crab has cholesterol. Cholesterol is
found only in foods of animal origin. It is not in fruits, vegetables
or vegetable oils.

Q. Do you reduce the cholesterol content of a piece of beef when you
trim the fat?

A. Yes! There is 20% more cholesterol in the fat of cooked beef than
in an equal weight of muscle.

Q. What does saturated, monounsaturated and polyunsaturated mean
when referring to fats?

A. These three terms have to do with the chemical structure of fatty
acids. Fatty acids are composed of chains of carbon atoms that have
sites for the attachment of hydrogen atoms. If these sites do not
have all the hydrogen atoms they can hold, there is a double bond
at that site.

Saturated fat—*all* the sites are filled with hydrogen atoms
*Mono*unsaturated—there is only *one* double bond
*Poly*unsaturated—there are *two or more* double bonds

Q. What are hydrogenated fats?

A. These are fats and oils that have been changed from their natural
liquid state to a solid state, such as margarines and shortenings.
They may be partially or completely hydrogenated. Avoid completely hydrogenated oils because they have become the same as
saturated fat. Partially hydrogenated oils may be used in moderation.

Q. Which of the following foods has the highest fat content?

- chocolate ice cream bar
- 2½ oz. lean pork chop
- 10 English walnuts

A. Gotcha?! The walnuts have the highest at 32 grams of fat. The pork chop has 8 grams while the ice cream has 19 grams.

Q. What foods are high in cholesterol?

A. Cholesterol is found in egg yolks, dairy products, meat, poultry, fish and shellfish. Egg yolks and organ meats (liver, kidney, sweetbread, brain) are particularly rich sources of cholesterol. Fish generally has less cholesterol than meat and poultry. Shellfish vary in cholesterol content but generally also have less cholesterol than meat and poultry.

Q. Which foods listed help lower your cholesterol?

- Liver
- Oat bran cereal
- Lentil soup
- Whole wheat bread
- Apples

A. The soluble fiber content of certain foods makes them valuable in helping to lower your cholesterol. Of the five listed foods, oat bran, lentils and apples all contain soluble fiber.

Q. Does my total cholesterol level increase my risk for having coronary heart disease?

A. Yes, if your total cholesterol level is in the range of:
- 200-239, you are classified as having "boderline-high" cholesterol and are at increased risk compared to those with lower levels.
- 240 and above, you have "high" cholesterol and your risk is even greater.

Q. What level should my cholesterol be?

A. The desirable cholesterol level is:

- Adults—less than 200
- Children—140 to 150

Q. If my cholesterol level is higher than it should be, what should I do to lower it?

A. Work with your doctor in doing the following things:

- Eat less high-fat foods, especially those high in saturated fat.
- Replace part of saturated fat in your diet with monounsaturated fat.
- Eat less high-cholesterol foods.
- Choose foods high in complex carbohydrates, especially those high in water soluble fiber.
- Do moderate aerobic exercise for at least 20-30 minutes, 3-4 times a week.
- Reduce your weight if over recommended weight.

Q. How long will it take to lower my cholesterol?

A. Generally your cholesterol level should begin to drop 2 to 3 weeks after you start on a cholesterol-lowering program. How rapidly and how low it drops, depends on:

a) How high it was to begin with
b) How well you follow the program
c) How responsive your body is to the cholesterol-lowering program

Q. How long do I need to follow a cholesterol-lowering program?

A. The program should be continued for life. While eating some foods high in saturated fat and cholesterol for one day or at one meal will not raise cholesterol levels, resuming old eating patterns, and putting on extra weight will.

Q. Will I need medication to lower my cholesterol?

A. Usually your doctor will have you follow a diet and exercise program for at least six months. If your cholesterol level has not dropped sufficiently, then you may be put on a medication along with your diet.

Q. Besides cutting down on saturated fat and cholesterol-laden foods, which of the steps below can a person take to reduce the chances of suffering a heart attack or stroke?

a) Exercise
b) Stop smoking
c) Keep blood pressure under control
d) All of the above

A. High blood pressure and smoking increase the risk of having a heart attack. To reduce the overall risk, most doctors suggest:

- If you smoke, stop

- If you don't exercise, start
- If your blood pressure is high, endeavor to lower it.

Therefore "d" is the best answer.

Q. What are the "good" HDLs and the "bad" LDLs I'm always hearing about?

A. Some cholesterol travels through the bloodstream in high density lipoproteins (HDLs). The HDLs carry cholesterol back to the liver for processing or removal from the body thereby preventing the accumulation of cholesterol in the artery walls. Hence the name, the "good" HDL cholesterol.

Cholesterol traveling in low density lipoproteins (LDLs) is transported from the liver to other parts of the body where it can be used. LDLs carry most of the cholesterol in the blood, and if all of it is not removed from the blood, cholesterol and fat can build up in the arteries contributing to atherosclerosis. This is why LDL cholesterol is often called "bad" LDL cholesterol.

Q. Are foods labeled "No Cholesterol" okay to buy and eat?

A. It depends. Many foods boasting "No Cholesterol" are high in saturated fat which is just as bad (if not worse for you) as cholesterol. Your best bet is to read the ingredient list on the label of the product to see what the fat content is.

Q. Is it ever too late to correct a cholesterol problem?

A. No! It is never too late to do something that may help your body chemistry function better and more efficiently.

Q. Is margarine safe to use if the label states, "Cholesterol Free"?

A. All margarines are "Cholesterol Free" because they are made from vegetable oils, not animal products. It's not a question of a food being safe or not, it's a matter of some foods being more beneficial than others in relation to the type of fat they contain, saturated or unsaturated. Use margarines which list a liquid vegetable oil first on the ingredient list. This indicates that the margarine is more unsaturated than saturated.

We wanted to say something cute at the end.
So, "cute"!

NOTES

COOKBOOK

When cooking to lower and control your cholesterol, remember it is most important to:

1. Avoid or decrease the saturated fat found mainly in:
   meats
   dairy foods
   tropical oils
2. Decrease the total fat content of foods prepared
3. Prepare more complex carbohydrate foods:
   whole grain cereals, pastas and breads
   vegetables
   fruits

What did the dough say to the baker?
"It's nice to be kneaded."

BREAKFAST

Breakfast is the most important meal of the day. It is the source of energy for getting your day off to a good start. Children should get a quarter of their daily food energy needs at breakfast. Any wholesome food can be eaten for breakfast, it doesn't have to be "traditional" breakfast food. Even something left over from dinner the night before, such as chicken, fruit salad, or a whole grain muffin and nonfat yogurt or a drink made from fresh fruit and nonfat milk.

Forget syrup for topping whole grain pancakes and waffles. Excess sugar intake possibly increases the triglyceride level, a no, no. Try using fresh or frozen fruits pureed and applesauce.

If you enjoy cereal for breakfast, stay away from prepared granola because it is high in fat.

APPLE, RAISIN OATBRAN CEREAL
serves 2

Ingredients:

2 cups water
⅛ tsp. salt
⅔ cup Quaker Oat Bran Cereal

½ apple diced
2 Tbs. raisins
½ tsp. cinnamon
2 Tbs. wheat germ

Preparation:

Combine in saucepan:
2 cups water
⅛ tsp. salt
Oat bran cereal
diced apple
2 Tbs. raisins
½ tsp. cinnamon
Bring to boil over high heat

Reduce heat
Cook 1 minute, stirring occasionally

Divide between 2 serving bowls
Sprinkle with wheat germ
Serve with skim milk

Estimated nutrition information per serving:

Total fat	3.1 grams	Monounsaturated fat	1.4 grams
Saturated fat	0.2 grams	Polyunsaturated fat	1.4 grams
		Cholesterol	0 milligrams

OAT PANCAKES
serves 4

Ingredients:

4 egg whites
2 Tbs. lite olive oil
1¾ cup orange juice
2 cups oat flour (Grind rolled oats in blender to make oat flour)

4 tsp. baking powder
1 tsp. cinnamon
¼ tsp. salt

Preparation:

Combine in medium bowl:
egg whites
2 Tbs. oil
orange juice

Combine in small bowl:
    flour
    4 tsp. baking powder
    1 tsp. cinnamon
    ¼ tsp. salt
Add to liquids, stir just until completely moistened
Cook on hot griddle, turning once

Delicious with applesauce

Estimated nutrition information per serving:

Total fat	9.8 grams	Monounsaturated fat	5.0 grams
Saturated fat	1.0 grams	Polyunsaturated fat	3.8 grams
		Cholesterol	0 milligram

CORNMEAL PANCAKES
serves 4

Ingredients:

1½ cups cornmeal	2 egg whites
2 tsp. baking powder	2 Tbs. canola oil
¼ tsp. salt	2 Tbs. concentrated fruit juice
	1 cup skim milk

Preparation:
Mix together in small bowl:
    cornmeal
    2 tsp. baking powder
    ¼ tsp. salt

Beat together in bowl until smooth:
    egg whites
    2 Tbs. canola oil
    2 Tbs. concentrated fruit juice
    skim milk

Add cornmeal mixture
Stir just till moistened
Cook on hot, lightly oiled griddle until golden brown, turn
    once.
Serve with applesauce or fruit only preserves

Estimated nutrition information per serving:

Total fat	8.0 grams	Monounsaturated fat	4.1 grams
Saturated fat	0.6 grams	Polyunsaturated fat	2.7 grams
		Cholesterol	1 milligrams

WAFFLES
serves 3

Ingredients:

2 cups whole wheat pastry flour
3 tsp. baking powder
1 tsp. sugar
¼ tsp. salt

1¾ cups skim milk
2 Tbs. canola oil
6 egg whites

Preparation:
Combine:
  flour
  3 tsp. baking powder
  1 tsp. sugar
  ¼ tsp. salt

Combine:
  skim milk
  2 Tbs. canola oil
  4 egg whites
Add to above and mixed till smooth
Beat till stiff:
  2 egg whites
Fold into mixture

Pour ⅓ cup onto hot waffle grill and cook
Serve with pureed fruit, delicious

Estimated nutrition information per serving:

Total fat	6.8 grams	Monounsaturated fat	3.3 grams
Saturated fat	0.8 grams	Polyunsaturated fat	2.1 grams
		Cholesterol	3 milligrams

BANANA BREAKFAST DRINK
2 cups

Ingredients:

1 cup skim milk
⅓ cup non-instant nonfat dry milk
2 ripe bananas

1 tsp. vanilla
1 cup cracked ice
⅛ tsp. nutmeg

Preparation:
Place in blender:
  skim milk
  dry milk
  ripe bananas, in 1" pieces

1 tsp. vanilla
cracked ice
Blend until smooth
Pour into 2 glasses
Sprinkle with nutmeg

Serve with oat bran muffins

Estimated nutrition information per serving:

Total fat	1.6 grams	Monounsaturated fat	0.1 grams
Saturated fat	0.4 grams	Polyunsaturated fat	0.1 grams
		Cholesterol	5 milligrams

SCRAMBLED EGGS PLUS
serves 2

Ingredients:

1 egg + 4 egg whites
1 Tbs. grated parmesan cheese
2 Tbs. water
salt & pepper
⅛ tsp. basil

2 tsp. olive oil
1 Tbs. chopped onion
¼ cup sliced mushrooms
1 Tbs. chopped green pepper
½ tomato, chopped

Preparation:

Combine in bowl:
    eggs
    1 Tbs. parmesan cheese
    2 Tbs. water
    salt & pepper to taste
    ⅛ tsp. basil, crushed

Saute in 2 tsp. olive oil in heavy skillet:
    ½ tomato, chopped
    1 Tbs. chopped onion
    ¼ cup sliced mushroom
    1 Tbs. chopped green pepper
Add egg mixture

Over medium heat, allow eggs to set slightly, pulling set edges
    inward and letting raw egg flow out.
Continue scrambling to desired doneness.

Estimated nutrition information per serving:

Total fat	4.1 grams	Monounsaturated fat	1.3 grams
Saturated fat	1.4 grams	Polyunsaturated fat	0.4 grams
		Cholesterol	105 milligrams

FRENCH TOAST
4 slices

Ingredients:

4 egg whites

⅓ cup orange juice

½ tsp. vanilla

4 slices whole wheat bread

Preparation:

In shallow dish, beat together:

egg whites

orange juice

½ tsp. vanilla

Spray skillet with nonstick vegetable coating

Heat skillet to medium heat

Dip slices of bread in egg mixture to coat both sides

Brown both sides of bread

Serve with pureed fruit, fruit only preserves or
unsweetened applesauce

Enjoy!

Estimated nutrition information per 2 slices:

Total fat	2.0 grams	Monounsaturated fat	0.8 grams
Saturated fat	0.8 grams	Polyunsaturated fat	0.6 grams
		Cholesterol	0 milligrams

SOUPS

A bowl of hearty soup with an oat bran muffin and homemade chunky applesauce make a great meal on a cold winter evening.

To add variety to your soups, include vegetables that you would not ordinarily eat.

BEAN SOUP
8–10 cups

Ingredients:

1 lb. bag of mixed beans
2 Tbs. broth or water
1 onion, chopped
½ green pepper, chopped
2 stalks celery with tops, chopped
2 tsp. paprika
2 quarts of defatted stock or water
1 bay leaf

1½ tsp. dill weed
¼ tsp. pepper
6 whole cloves
1 tsp. oregano
10 oz. corn
1 lb. can of tomatoes
1 large potato, chopped
2 carrots, chopped

Preparation:

Place beans in large pot:
Cover with water to 2″ above beans
Bring to boil, boil 2 minutes
Remove from heat, cover and let stand 1 hour

Saute in broth or water in dutch oven:
    chopped onions
    chopped green peppers
    chopped celery
    2 tsp. paprika

Add:
    drained beans
    bay leaf
    1½ tsp. dill weed
    ¼ tsp. pepper
    6 cloves
    1 tsp. oregano

Simmer for 1–1½ hours

Add:
    corn
    tomatoes
    chopped carrots
    chopped potato
Simmer till vegetables and beans tender

If desire a thicker soup:
    remove some potato and vegetables from soup
    place in blender
    blend till smooth
    stir back into soup

For a fuller flavor, make a day ahead

Estimated nutrition information per serving, 1 cup

Total fat	2.4 grams	Monounsaturated fat	1.2 grams
Saturated fat	0.3 grams	Polyunsaturated fat	0.7 grams
		Cholesterol	0 milligrams

CORN CHOWDER DELIGHT
serves 8

Ingredients:

3 onions, diced	½ tsp. pepper
1 Tbs. olive oil	¼ tsp. thyme
1 cup celery, chopped	32 oz. frozen corn
2 cups defatted broth or water	4 cups skim milk
6 potatoes, peeled and chopped	parsley (optional)
1 tsp. salt	paprika (optional)

Preparation:
Add to heated large saucepan or soup kettle and saute:
　1 Tbs. olive oil
　1 Tbs. water
　diced onions
　chopped celery
Add:
　2 cups broth or water
　chopped potatoes
　1 tsp. salt
　½ tsp. pepper
　¼ tsp. thyme

Cook until potatoes tender, about 15 minutes
Mash potatoes slightly
Add:
　32 oz. corn
　4 cups milk
Simmer but do not boil, until corn cooked, 5 to 10 minutes
Serve garnished with parsley and/or paprika

Estimated nutrition information per serving, 1 cup:

Total fat	2.6 grams	Monounsaturated fat	1.4 grams
Saturated fat	0.5 grams	Polyunsaturated fat	0.4 grams
		Cholesterol	3 milligrams

MINESTRONE
10–12 cups

Ingredients:

1 Tbs. olive oil
1 onion, chopped
1½ cup celery, chopped
1 clove garlic, minced
½ cup chopped parsley
salt & pepper to taste
2 bay leaves
1 tsp. oregano
2 tsp. basil
½ tsp. rosemary
5 cups crushed tomatoes

¼ cup barley
3 cups + of chopped vegetables;
   carrot, corn, green beans,
   green pepper, peas, potato
1 cup lima beans
1 cup canned garbanzo beans
1 cup whole wheat macaroni
¼ cup chopped zucchini
¼ cup chopped cabbage
¼ cup sliced mushrooms
parmesan cheese

Preparation:

Heat in heavy soup pot:
   3 Tbs. water
   1 Tbs. olive oil
Add and saute until soft:
   chopped onion
   chopped celery
   minced garlic

Add:
   chopped parsley
   salt & pepper to taste
   2 bay leaves
   1 tsp. oregano, crushed
   2 tsp. basil, crushed
   ½ tsp. rosemary, crushed
   crushed tomatoes
   ¼ cup barley

Bring to boil over medium heat
Reduce heat and simmer while you prepare vegetables
Stir occasionally

Add:
   3 cups chopped vegetables
   lima beans
   garbanzo beans
   macaroni
Bring to boil
Reduce heat and simmer until vegetables almost cooked
Stir occasionally

Add:
    chopped zucchini
    sliced mushrooms
    chopped cabbage
Simmer 5–10 minutes

Taste to check seasoning, adjusting as needed
If soup too thick, add some tomato juice, broth or water

Sprinkle each serving with 1 tsp. parmesan cheese

Estimated nutrition information per serving, 1 cup:

Total fat	3.5 grams	Monounsaturated fat	1.4 grams
Saturated fat	0.7 grams	Polyunsaturated fat	0.6 grams
		Cholesterol	1.5 milligrams

LENTIL SOUP
serves 4

Ingredients:

4 cups defatted stock or water
1 cup lentils
½ cup brown rice
salt to taste
1 tsp. basil
½ tsp. tarragon
1 Tbs. olive oil

1 onion, sliced
1 green pepper, diced
2 carrots, diced
2 stalks celery & leaves, diced
1 clove garlic, minced
1 lb. fresh or canned tomatoes
1 Tbs. miso (optional)

Preparation:

Put in 2 quart saucepan:
  stock or water
  lentils
  brown rice
  salt to taste
  1 tsp. basil, crushed
  ½ tsp. tarragon, crushed
Simmer 45 minutes

Heat in soup pot:
  1 Tbs. oil
Saute:
  sliced onion
  diced pepper
  diced carrots
  diced celery
  minced garlic

Add:
  tomatoes
  rice and lentil mixture
Simmer 15 minutes

Add 5 minutes before serving:
  1 Tbs. miso which has been thoroughly mixed with ½ cup
  soup

Stir well, and do not let soup boil

Serve with green salad and whole grain bread

Estimated nutrition information per serving, 1 cup:

Total fat	4.9 grams	Monounsaturated fat	2.9 grams
Saturated fat	0.7 grams	Polyunsaturated fat	0.8 grams
		Cholesterol	0 milligrams

SALADS

WALDORF SALAD
serves 6

Ingredients:
3 medium apples, chopped
2 tsp. lemon juice
¼ cup raisins
½ cup celery, chopped
¼ cup chopped pecans
½ cup cut orange sections

⅛ tsp. nutmeg
⅛ tsp. cinnamon
¼ cup plain low fat (1%) yogurt
2 tsp. concentrated apple juice
1 Tbs. sunflower seeds

Preparation:
Place in bowl:
    chopped apples
    lemon juice
Toss to coat apples
Add:
    ¼ cup raisins
    ½ cup chopped celery
    ¼ cup chopped pecans
    ½ cup cut oranges
    ⅛ tsp. nutmeg
    ⅛ tsp. cinnamon
Toss lightly to mix

Combine:
    ¼ cup plain yogurt
    2 tsp. thawed apple juice
Mix with fruit mixture
Toss together lightly
Chill
Serve on bed of lettuce
Sprinkle with sunflower seeds

Estimated nutrition information per serving:

Total fat	3.9 grams	Monounsaturated fat	2.1 grams
Saturated fat	0.5 grams	Polyunsaturated fat	1.2 grams
		Cholesterol	1 milligram

SUNSHINE SALAD
serves 6

Ingredients:
1¾ cups orange juice
2 envelopes unflavored gelatin
2 Tbs. concentrated pineapple juice

¼ cup lemon juice
1½ cups carrot cut in 1" pieces
8 oz. crushed pineapple

Preparation:
  Pour into 5 cup blender:
    ½ cup cold orange juice
  Sprinkle on top of juice and let stand 3–4 minutes:
    2 envelopes gelatin
  Heat and add to blender:
    1¼ cups orange juice
  Blend at low speed till gelatin completely dissolved, about 4
    minutes
  Add and blend at high speed till blended:
    2 Tbs. concentrated pineapple juice
    ¼ cup lemon juice
  Add and chop in blender:
    1½ cup carrot pieces
  Pour into 8″ square glass dish
  Stir in: 8 oz. crushed pineapple in own juice
  Chill till firm

Estimated nutrition information per serving:

Total fat	0 grams	Monounsaturated fat	0 grams
Saturated fat	0 grams	Polyunsaturated fat	0 grams
		Cholesterol	0 milligrams

CALICO SALAD
serves 6

Ingredients:

1 cup cooked potatoes, diced	2 Tbs. onions, chopped
1 cup cooked carrots, diced	2 Tbs. fresh parsley, chopped
1 cup cooked peas	¼ cup light French dressing
¼ cup red sweet pepper, chopped	½ head leaf lettuce
¼ cup cauliflower, chopped	

Preparation:
  Combine in large bowl:
    all above ingredients except lettuce & dressing
  Chill 1 hour
  In another large bowl:
    break lettuce into bite-size pieces
  Add:
    chilled vegetables
    dressing
  Toss lightly

Estimated nutrition information per serving:

Total fat	1.5 grams	Monounsaturated fat	0.2 grams
Saturated fat	0.2 grams	Polyunsaturated fat	0.8 grams
		Cholesterol	0 milligrams

BEAN SALAD
serves 6

Ingredients:
1 carrot, sliced cooked crisp tender
16 oz can kidney or pink beans, drained
16 oz. can white beans, drained
¼ cup green pepper, chopped
¼ cup celery, sliced
2 Tbs. olive oil

2 Tbs. white wine vinegar
¼ tsp. sugar
⅛ tsp. salt
⅛ tsp. oregano
⅛ tsp. basil
dash of pepper
Leaf lettuce for 6

Preparation:
Combine in bowl:
  cooked carrot
  kidney or pink beans
  white beans
  chopped pepper
  chopped celery

Combine in small jar:
  2 Tbs. olive oil
  2 Tbs. white wine vinegar
  ¼ tsp. sugar
  ⅛ tsp. salt
  ⅛ tsp. oregano, crushed
  ⅛ tsp. basil, crushed
  dash pepper
Cover and shake till thoroughly mixed
Pour over bean mixture
Toss to coat salad items

Cover, refrigerate at least 4 hours or overnight
Drain dressing from beans and reserve
Serve beans with lettuce
Serve reserved dressing to be used as desired

Estimated nutrition information per serving:

Total fat	4.9 grams	Monounsaturated fat	3.5 grams
Saturated fat	0.7 grams	Polyunsaturated fat	0.6 grams
		Cholesterol	0 milligrams

LENTIL SALAD
serves 4

Ingredients:

½ cup red lentils
1 Tbs. chopped scallions
3 Tbs. fresh parsley, chopped
¼ cup carrots, sliced thin
green leaf lettuce
3 Tbs. broth or water

1 Tbs. olive oil
1½ tsp. tarragon vinegar
¼ tsp. dry mustard
salt
pepper

Preparation:

Cook till tender, about 30 minutes:
    ½ cup lentils with 1½ cups water
Drain and cool lentils
Mix with cooled lentils:
    chopped scallions
    chopped parsley
    sliced carrots

Mix together in jar for dressing:
    1 Tbs. olive oil
    3 Tbs. broth or water
    1½ tsp. tarragon vinegar
    ¼ tsp. dry mustard
    salt & pepper to taste
Shake well
Pour over lentil mixture

Chill
To serve, spoon onto bed of lettuce

Estimated nutrition information per serving:

Total fat	3.8 grams	Monounsaturated fat	2.6 grams
Saturated fat	0.5 grams	Polyunsaturated fat	0.4 grams
		Cholesterol	0 milligrams

VEGETABLE SALAD
serves 6–8

Ingredients:

1½ lbs. broccoli
3 carrots, diagonally sliced, thin
1 can sliced beets
1 small head cauliflower
1 red onion, sliced thin in rings
1 Tbs. olive oil

3 Tbs. tarragon vinegar
2 Tbs. broth or water
3 fresh basil leaves
2 garlic cloves, mashed
pepper
1 Tbs. dijon mustard

Preparation:

Separate broccoli flowerets from stems, cut stems on diagonal
   in ¼" slices
Break cauliflower into pieces
Steam till crisp tender:
   broccoli
   carrots
   cauliflower
Rinse under cold water
Place in large bowl:
   carrots
   cauliflower
   beets
   onion cut in rings

Combine in jar:
   1 Tbs. olive oil
   2 Tbs. broth or water
   3 Tbs. tarragon vinegar
   3 fresh basil leaves
   2 mashed garlic cloves
   pepper to taste
   1 Tbs. mustard
Put on lid and shake well
Pour over vegetables in bowl
Toss lightly

Cover and refrigerate 3–4 hours
Add ½ hour before serving:
   broccoli

Estimated nutrition information per serving:

Total fat	2.3 grams	Monounsaturated fat	1.3 grams
Saturated fat	0.3 grams	Polyunsaturated fat	0.4 grams
		Cholesterol	0 milligrams

ENTREES

The following entrees (main dishes) range from traditional meat and chicken dishes to not-so-familiar tofu (soybean product) dishes. You may wonder how you will be eating sufficient protein if there is no meat, poultry or fish as part of a meal. Grains, nuts & seeds (sesame, sunflower, etc) and legumes (beans, peas and lentils) all contain protein and when combined or served together make a complete protein. An excellent legume protein is tofu which comes from soybeans. It is high in protein, low in saturated fat and very versatile.

CHILI AND CORN
serves 6

Ingredients:

3 Tbs. vegetable broth or water
1 onion, chopped
1 clove garlic, minced
4 oz. can green chili peppers, diced

2 cups crushed tomatoes
1½ cups whole corn

4 cups cooked kidney beans
¼ tsp. chili powder
¼ tsp. cumin powder
1 tsp. salt
1 tsp. oregano
½ tsp. dry mustard

Preparation:

Cook in Dutch oven till onion soft:
3 Tbs. vegetable broth or water
1 chopped onion
1 minced garlic clove

Add:
diced chilie peppers
crushed tomatoes
corn
cooked kidney beans
¼ tsp. chili powder
¼ tsp. cumin powder
1 tsp. salt
1 tsp. oregano, crushed
½ tsp. dry mustard
Cover and simmer 30 minutes

If too thin:
remove some beans and blend in blender
stir back into chili
or
remove lid and cook about 10 minutes to reduce liquid

Estimated nutrition information per serving:

Total fat	0.7 grams	Monounsaturated fat	0.1 grams
Saturated fat	0.1 grams	Polyunsaturated fat	0.5 grams
		Cholesterol	0 milligrams

LASAGNA
serves 10–12

Ingredients:

5¼ cups Italian tomato sauce
6 Tbs. dried parsley
2 tsp. garlic powder
1 tsp. onion powder
1¼ tsp. oregano
1¼ tsp. basil

8 large whole wheat lasagna
   noodles
2⅓ cups uncreamed low fat
   cottage cheese
4 egg whites, beaten stiffly
1 cup nonfat buttermilk
¾ cup grated sapsago cheese

Preparation:

Combine in saucepan and cook 20–30 minutes:
   5¼ cups Italian tomato sauce
   2 Tbs. dried parsley
   2 tsp. garlic powder
   1 tsp. onion powder
   1¼ tsp. oregano
   1¼ tsp. basil
Begin heating water for cooking noodles
In bowl combine with fork:
   cottage cheese
   buttermilk

Add:
   grated sapsago cheese
   4 Tbs. parsley
Fold in:
   egg whites

Refrigerate until noodles and sauce ready
Cook noodles according to package directions
Drain noodles
In a large shallow baking dish repeat layers of:
   tomato sauce
   noodles
   cheese
   end with sauce on top
Bake at 375° for about 1 hour or until thoroughly cooked and
   bubbly

Estimated nutrition information per serving, ¹⁄₁₂ of whole:

Total fat	2.6 grams	Monounsaturated fat	0.8 grams
Saturated fat	1.6 grams	Polyunsaturated fat	0.2 grams
		Cholesterol	13.0 milligrams

BAKED MACARONI AND BEANS
serves 6

Ingredients:

1 medium zucchini
1 medium onion, diced
½ lb. mushrooms, quartered
3 Tbs. water or defatted broth
1 28-oz. can tomatoes
8 oz. medium sized shell macaroni

1½ cups nonfat milk
¼ tsp. salt
¾ tsp. dried basil, crushed
½ cup grated Parmesan cheese
10 oz. Fordhook lima beans

Preparation:

Cut:
    zucchini lengthwise, then crosswise in ¼" slices
Heat oven to 350°
Cook in 12" skillet over medium-high heat till tender-crisp:
    3 Tbs. water or broth
    zucchini
    diced onions
    quartered mushrooms

Add:
    tomatoes with their liquid
    macaroni
    milk
    ¼ tsp. salt
    ¾ tsp. crushed basil
Stir to break up tomatoes
Heat over high heat to boiling
Spoon macaroni mixture into shallow 2 quart casserole

Cover with foil
Bake 30 minutes

Remove casserole from oven and stir in:
    Parmesan cheese
    lima beans
Cover, continue baking for 20 minutes, till:
    beans tender
    casserole hot

Estimated nutrition information per serving:

Total fat	4.9 grams	Monounsaturated fat	1.0 grams
Saturated fat	2.0 grams	Polyunsaturated fat	0.9 grams
		Cholesterol	8.0 milligrams

RICE AND LENTILS
serves 4–6

Ingredients:

1 Tbs. tomato paste
¼ tsp. cinnamon
¼ cup lentils
2½ cups vegetable stock or water
¼ tsp. saffron
2 Tbs defatted broth or water
½ medium onion, chopped

½ green pepper, chopped
1 cup brown rice
½ tsp. salt
½ cup sunflower seeds or
    almonds, chopped
½ cup raisins

Preparation:

Combine in small bowl:
   1 Tbs. tomato paste
   ¼ tsp. cinnamon
   lentils
   vegetable stock or water
   ¼ tsp. saffron

Saute in 2 Tbs. defatted broth or water:
   chopped onion
   chopped pepper
Add and stir for several minutes:
   rice
   lentil mixture
Bring to boil, cover tightly
Reduce heat to low
Simmer for 30 minutes

Remove from heat and stir in:
   ½ tsp. salt
   sunflower seed or almonds
   raisins
Spray baking dish with non stick spray
Place in dish:
   1 Tbs. hot water
   rice mixture
Cover
Bake for 20–30 minutes at 350°

Estimated nutrition information per serving, ⅙ of whole with sunflower
   seeds:

Total fat	5.5 grams	Monounsaturated fat	1.2 grams
Saturated fat	0.6 grams	Polyunsaturated fat	3.4 grams
		Cholesterol	0 milligrams

TOFU AND PEPPERS
serves 4

Ingredients:

2 Tbs. water or defatted broth
2 garlic cloves, minced
½ tsp. ground ginger
1 carrot cut in ¼" slices
2 cups broccoli, cut in 1" pieces
1 sweet red pepper, cut in 1" pieces

1 green pepper, cut in 1" pieces
6 scallions, chopped
2 Tbs. soy sauce
1 Tbs. vinegar
½ lb. firm tofu, cut in small cubes

Preparation:

Heat in heavy skillet or wok:
   2 Tbs. water or defatted broth
Add:
   2 garlic cloves, minced
   ½ tsp. ground ginger
   1 carrot cut in ¼" slices
   2 cups broccoli, cut in 1" pieces
Stir-fry for 2–3 minutes

Add:
   1 sweet red pepper cut in 1" pieces
   1 green pepper cut in 1" pieces
Stir-fry for 3–4 minutes
Add:
   6 chopped scallions
Stir-fry 1 minute

Add and stir gently:
   2 Tbs. soy sauce
   1 Tbs. vinegar
   ½ lb. cubed firm tofu
Cover and steam over low heat for 5–7 minutes
Enjoy with candle light and soft music

Estimated nutrition information per serving:

Total fat	3.7 grams	Monounsaturated fat	0.7 grams
Saturated fat	0.5 grams	Polyunsaturated fat	2.2 grams
		Cholesterol	0 milligrams

TOFU AND VEGETABLES, STIR-FRIED
serves 4–6

Ingredients:

2 Tbs. water or defatted broth
2 garlic cloves, minced
½ tsp. ginger
2 medium carrots, cut in thin slices
1 cup cut green beans
2 sweet red peppers, cut in 1" pieces

1 stalk celery, cut in 1" pieces
1 small onion, sliced
2 Tbs. soy sauce
2 tsp. vinegar
¾ lb. tofu, cut in ½" cubes

Preparation:

Heat in large skillet or wok:
2 Tbs. water or defatted broth

Add and stir fry for 2 minutes:
2 garlic cloves, minced
½ tsp. ginger
2 medium carrots cut in thin slices
1 cup cut green beans

Add and stir fry for 2 minutes:
2 sweet red peppers, cut in 1" pieces
1 stalk celery cut in 1" pieces

Add and stir fry 1 minute:
1 small onion, sliced

Add and stir together:
2 Tbs. soy sauce
2 tsp. vinegar
¾ lb. tofu cut in ½" cubes
Cover and steam over low heat for 5–7 minutes
Serve immediately

Estimated nutrition information per serving, ⅙ of whole:

Total fat	3.3 grams	Monounsaturated fat	0.6 grams
Saturated fat	0.5 grams	Polyunsaturated fat	1.9 grams
		Cholesterol	0 milligrams

A fat kitchen, a lean will.—Benjamin Franklin, Poor Richard, 1733

SALMON AND ASPARAGUS WITH PASTA
serves 4

Ingredients:

1 tsp. canola oil
2 scallions, chopped
1 garlic clove, minced
½ tsp. fresh ginger, minced
½ can (14 oz.) water packed
   artichoke hearts, diced
½ cup defatted chicken broth

2 Tbs. fresh lemon juice
½ lb. thin spinach spaghetti
1½ cups asparagus pieces or peas
6½ oz. canned salmon, drained,
   rinsed, broken into large chunks
pepper to taste
4 tsp. Parmesan cheese

Preparation:

Begin heating water to cook pasta
Saute for 1 minute in 1 tsp. canola oil:
   chopped scallions
   minced garlic
   ½ tsp. minced ginger

Add:
   artichokes
   broth
   1 Tbs. lemon juice
Simmer 1 minute

Add and cook 2 to 4 minutes:
   cut asparagus or peas

Add and toss gently:
   salmon
Season with:
   pepper
Cook pasta according to directions
Drain and toss with:
   1 Tbs. lemon juice
Divide pasta among 4 plates
Top with salmon mixture
Sprinkle with Parmesan cheese

Estimated nutrition information per serving:

Total fat	5.7 grams	Monounsaturated fat	1.7 grams
Saturated fat	1.0 grams	Polyunsaturated fat	1.8 grams
		Cholesterol	19 milligrams

SHRIMP CREOLE
serves 4

Ingredients:

1 lb. cooked shrimp	½ cup water
2 Tbs. water	¼ tsp. salt
½ cup onions, chopped	pepper to taste
½ cup green pepper, sliced thin	1 tsp. Worcestershire sauce
½ cup celery, diced	⅛ tsp. garlic powder
16 oz. tomato sauce	¼ tsp. chili powder
1 Tbs. vinegar	1 bay leaf
1 tsp. sugar	1 Tbs. horseradish
	2 cups cooked brown rice

Preparation:

Heat in large saucepan:
>   2 Tbs. water

Add and saute till tender, stirring frequently:
>   ½ cup chopped onions
>   ½ cup sliced peppers
>   ½ cup diced celery
>   add small amount of water if necessary to prevent drying

Add:
>   16 oz. tomato sauce
>   1 Tbs. vinegar
>   1 tsp. sugar
>   ½ cup water
>   ¼ tsp. salt
>   pepper to taste
>   1 tsp. Worcestershire sauce
>   ⅛ tsp. garlic powder
>   ¼ tsp. chili powder
>   1 bay leaf
>   1 Tbs. horseradish

Heat until sauce just begins to boil, remove bay leaf
Reduce heat, add shrimp and heat through
Serve over brown rice
No finger lick'n please!

Estimated nutrition information per serving:

Total fat	2.0 grams	Monounsaturated fat	0.5 grams
Saturated fat	0.5 grams	Polyunsaturated fat	0.8 grams
		Cholesterol	171 milligrams

BAKED FLOUNDER
serves 2–4

Ingredients:

1 lb. fillets of flounder	1 tsp. canola oil
salt	pepper
paprika	¼ tsp. thyme
2 Tbs. Swiss cheese (optional)	

Preparation:

Place in lightly oiled baking dish:
   fillets
Brush with:
   1 tsp. canola oil
Sprinkle with:
   salt
   pepper
   paprika
   ¼ tsp. thyme
   2 Tbs. grated Swiss cheese (optional)
Bake at 400° for 10 to 15 minutes

Estimated nutrition information per serving:

Total fat	3.3 grams	Monounsaturated fat	1.1 grams
Saturated fat	1.0 grams	Polyunsaturated fat	0.9 grams
		Cholesterol	70 milligrams

TURKEY CHILI
serves 10–12

Ingredients:

1¼ lb. lean ground turkey
2 large onions, chopped
2 15–19 oz. cans kidney beans
2 15–19 oz. cans pinto beans
1 28 oz. can peeled Italian tomatoes
1 14½ oz. can stewed tomatoes

1 large green pepper, chopped
2–4 Tbs. chili powder
1 tsp. garlic powder
1 tsp. oregano
⅛ tsp. ground red pepper
⅛ tsp. pepper

Preparation:

Cook in Dutch Oven:
   ground turkey till not pink
   chopped onions till tender
Drain off fat

Stir in:
   beans, reserve liquid to add later if desire thinner chili
   cut up Italian tomatoes
   stewed tomatoes
   chopped pepper
   2–4 Tbs. chili powder
   1 tsp. garlic powder
   1 tsp. oregano, crushed
   ⅛ tsp. ground red pepper (optional)
   ⅛ tsp. pepper
Bring to boil
Reduce heat, simmer uncovered for 1¼ hours or until desired
   consistency
Stir occasionally

Estimated nutrition information per serving, ¹⁄₁₂ of whole:

Total fat	4.0 grams	Monounsaturated fat	0.7 grams
Saturated fat	1.2 grams	Polyunsaturated fat	1.2 grams
		Cholesterol	33 milligrams

TURKEY COLOMBO
serves 8

Ingredients:

⅓ cup oat bran
1 tsp. oregano, crushed
¼ tsp. garlic powder
¼ tsp. onion powder
¼ tsp. pepper, freshly ground
1½ lbs. turkey cutlet, cut in
  serving size pieces

½ cup skim milk
½ lb. fresh mushrooms, sliced
3 Tbs. tomato paste
¼ cup marsala or sherry
2 Tbs. fresh parsley, chopped

Preparation:

Mix together in shallow dish:
  oat bran
  1 tsp. crushed oregano
  ¼ tsp. garlic powder
  ¼ tsp. onion powder
  ¼ tsp. pepper

Pour into another shallow dish:
  skim milk
Dip turkey into milk then into oat bran mixture
Broil until golden on both sides

Combine:
  sliced mushrooms
  tomato paste
  wine
Pour over cutlets
Simmer 10 minutes
Serve garnished with parsley

Estimated nutrition information per serving:

Total fat	3.3 grams	Monounsaturated fat	0.5 grams
Saturated fat	0.9 grams	Polyunsaturated fat	0.7 grams
		Cholesterol	59 milligrams

TURKEY STROGANOFF
serves 4

Ingredients:

1 lb. turkey breast slices
¾ lb. fresh mushrooms, sliced
1 medium onion, sliced
1 green pepper, sliced thin
1 cup plain nonfat yogurt, room
    temp.

2 Tbs. flour
½ tsp. thyme
½ tsp. garlic salt
2 tsp. prepared mustard
paprika
1 tsp. prepared horseradish

Preparation:

Cut meat diagonally across grain in 1" wide strips
In skillet, brown strips quickly in:
    2 Tbs. water
Push browned meat to one side and add:
    sliced mushrooms
    sliced onion
    sliced pepper
Cook till just tender

Combine:
    yogurt
    2 Tbs. flour
    ½ tsp. thyme
    ½ tsp. garlic salt
    2 tsp. prepared mustard
    1 tsp. prepared horseradish

Add to skillet, stirring constantly till thickens slightly and
    bubbles
Serve over hot cooked noodles, sprinkle with paprika

Estimated nutrition information per serving:

Total fat	3.3 grams	Monounsaturated fat	1.9 grams
Saturated fat	0.8 grams	Polyunsaturated fat	0.4 grams
		Cholesterol	36 milligrams

BARBECUED CHICKEN
serves 12

Ingredients:

6 chicken breasts cut in half,
  skinned
3 bay leaves
3 large garlic cloves, quartered
10 peppercorns

2 cups tomato sauce
2 Tbs. worcestershire sauce
1 Tbs. white vinegar
2 Tbs. brown sugar

Preparation:

Place in dutch oven:
  chicken breasts, skin and fat removed
  3 bay leaves
  3 large garlic cloves
  10 peppercorns
  water to cover chicken
Bring to boil, then simmer for 30 minutes
Remove chicken and seasonings from stock, refrigerate or freeze stock for later use in soups, cooking rice, etc.

Combine for sauce:
  2 cups tomato sauce
  2 Tbs. worcestershire sauce
  1 Tbs. white vinegar
  2 Tbs. brown sugar

Coat chicken pieces with sauce
Broil in oven or on grill until sauce is brown and chicken thoroughly heated
Baste chicken with sauce while cooking

Estimated nutrition information per serving:

Total fat	3.1 grams	Monounsaturated fat	1.1 grams
Saturated fat	0.9 grams	Polyunsaturated fat	0.7 grams
		Cholesterol	73 milligrams

CHICKEN A LA KING
serves 4

Ingredients:

1 Tbs. canola oil
2 Tbs. chopped green pepper
2 Tbs. chopped onion
¼ cup celery, diced
2 Tbs. flour

½ tsp. salt
2 cups skim milk
2½ cups cooked chicken
    breast, chopped
2 Tbs. chopped pimientos
¾ cup sliced mushrooms

Preparation:

Heat in skillet or stove top casserole:
    1 Tbs. canola oil

Add and saute lightly:
    2 Tbs. chopped green pepper
    2 Tbs. chopped onion
    ¼ cup diced celery
Stir in till well blended:
    2 Tbs. flour
    ½ tsp. salt
Stir while adding:
    2 cups skim milk
Cook and stir until smooth and slightly thickened

Add:
    2½ cups, chopped chicken
    2 Tbs. chopped red pimientos
    ¾ cup sliced mushrooms
Stir until well mixed
Heat thoroughly

May be served over:
    biscuit
    toast
    brown rice
    noodles
Eat and enjoy as if a king!

Estimated nutrition information per serving:

Total fat	7.1 grams	Monounsaturated fat	3.1 grams
Saturated fat	1.3 grams	Polyunsaturated fat	1.9 grams
		Cholesterol	76 milligrams

OVEN FRIED CHICKEN TERIYAKI
serves 12

Must be partly prepared the day before or morning of day served

Ingredients:

1½ cups soya sauce (salt reduced)
2½ cups unsweetened pineapple juice
2¼ tsp. garlic powder
½ cup cornmeal
1 tsp. onion powder
½ tsp. poultry seasoning

1½ cups lemon juice
1 Tbs. ground ginger
6 large halved chicken breasts
½ cup oat bran
½ tsp. paprika
¼ tsp. pepper
2 Tbs. sapsago cheese

Preparation:

Combine in shallow baking dish for marinade:
   1½ cups soya sauce
   1½ cups lemon juice
   2½ cups unsweetened pineapple juice
   1 Tbs. ground ginger
   1½ tsp. garlic powder
Remove skin and fat from chicken
Cut halved breast in half again = 12 pieces
Marinate chicken in marinade for several hours or over night in refrigerator
When ready to cook chicken, combine:
   ½ cup cornmeal
   ½ cup oat bran
   1 tsp. onion powder
   ¾ tsp. garlic powder
   ½ tsp. paprika
   ½ tsp. poultry seasoning
   ¼ tsp. pepper
   2 Tbs. grated sapsago cheese
Remove chicken from marinade
Coat well with cornmeal oat mixture
Arrange chicken on nonstick baking sheet
Cover with aluminum foil, except for the first 10 and last 10 minutes of cooking
Preheat oven to 350°
Bake for 1 hour or until tender

Estimated nutrition information per serving:

Total fat	3.7 grams	Monounsaturated fat	1.1 grams
Saturated fat	0.9 grams	Polyunsaturated fat	0.7 grams
		Cholesterol	74 milligrams

VEGETABLES

Vegetables are complex carbohydrates and are excellent sources of soluble fiber. To retain their vitamins and minerals, try steaming vegetables rather than boiling them and throwing many of their nutrients down the drain with the cooking water.

PICKLED BEETS
serves 4

Ingredients:
1 lb. beets	¼ tsp. mustard seeds
¼ cup vinegar	1 tsp. prepared mustard
⅛ tsp. salt	½ tsp. basil, crushed
4 cloves	dash of pepper

Preparation:
Slip into boiling water:
  scrubbed beets
Cook till tender, about 30 to 40 minutes
Hold cooked beet under running cool water and slip off its skin
While beets cooking, combine:
  1 cup water
  ¼ cup vinegar
  ⅛ tsp. salt
  4 cloves
  ¼ tsp. mustard seeds
  1 tsp. prepared mustard
  ½ tsp. crushed basil
  dash of pepper
Slice cooked beets into shallow dish
Pour vinegar mixture over beets
Chill for at least 3 hours

Estimated nutrition information per serving:
Total fat	0 grams	Monounsaturated fat	0 grams
Saturated fat	0 grams	Polyunsaturated fat	0 grams
		Cholesterol	0 milligrams

GREEN BEANS AND TOMATOES
serves 6

Ingredients:
20 oz. whole green beans	⅛ tsp. salt
1 Tbs. water or broth	½ tsp. marjoram, crushed
¼ cup onion, chopped	1 tsp. tarragon, crushed
4 medium tomatoes, chopped	

Preparation:
Cook in saucepan:
  beans

Add to skillet over medium heat:
  1 Tbs. water or broth
  chopped onions
Cook 5 minutes
Add:
  chopped tomatoes
  ⅛ tsp. salt
  ½ tsp. crushed marjoram
  1 tsp. crushed tarragon
Cover and simmer 10 minutes
Add:
  cooked beans
Cover, simmer till thoroughly heated

Estimated nutrition information per serving:

Total fat	0 grams	Monounsaturated fat	0 grams
Saturated fat	0 grams	Polyunsaturated fat	0 grams
		Cholesterol	0 milligrams

DEVILED GREEN BEANS
serves 5

Ingredients:
  1 lb. whole green beans
  ½ cup low fat plain yogurt
  1 tsp. prepared mustard
  Hot pepper sauce to taste

  1 tsp. Worcestershire sauce
  ¼ tsp. pepper
  Cayenne pepper to taste

Preparation:
  Cook beans and drain
  Combine in small bowl:
    yogurt
    1 tsp. mustard
    hot pepper sauce to taste
    1 tsp. Worcestershire sauce
    ¼ tsp. pepper
    Cayenne pepper to taste
  Pour over hot beans, serve immediately
Hm-Hm Good!

Estimated nutrition information per serving:

Total fat	0.7 grams	Monounsaturated fat	0.1 grams
Saturated fat	0.3 grams	Polyunsaturated fat	0.2 grams
		Cholesterol	1 milligram

BAKED SQUASH
serves 3–4

Ingredients:
1 acorn squash
Butter Buds

Cinnamon
1¼ cups applesauce

Preparation:
Wash, cut in half, remove seeds from:
  squash
Place in glass baking dish:
  squash, cut side down
Bake at 350° for 35 minutes
Turn squash over and continue baking for 25 minutes or till
  tender

Heat in saucepan:
  applesauce
Sprinkle on inside of squash:
  Butter Buds
  cinnamon to taste
Spoon into squash:
  hot applesauce

Variation: May remove cooked squash from shell and mix all
  ingredients together, then serve.

Estimated nutrition information per serving:
Total fat   0.8 grams
Saturated fat 0.3 grams

Monounsaturated fat 0.1 grams
Polyunsaturated fat 0.4 grams
Cholesterol   0 milligrams

CARROTS, CAULIFLOWER AND PEPPERS
serves 4

Ingredients:
2 Tbs. broth or water
2 cups carrots, diagonally cut
¼ cup green bell pepper, chopped

2 cups cauliflower, small pieces
¼ tsp. tarragon, crushed
¼ tsp. rosemary, crushed

Preparation:
Heat in heavy skillet over med-high heat:
  2 Tbs. broth or water

Add, stir for 2 minutes:
  cut carrots

Add, stir 1 minute:
    chopped peppers
Add, stir 2 minutes:
    cut cauliflower
    ¼ tsp. crushed tarragon
    ¼ tsp. crushed rosemary
Cover and cook over low heat about 10 minutes or till
    vegetables tender

Estimated nutrition information per serving:

Total fat	0.2 grams	Monounsaturated fat	0.0 grams
Saturated fat	0.1 grams	Polyunsaturated fat	0.1 grams
		Cholesterol	0 milligrams

CHEESY CAULIFLOWER
serves 4

Ingredients:

3 cups cauliflower flowerets	2 Tbs. fresh parsley, chopped
½ cup low fat cottage cheese	1 Tbs. Parmesan cheese, grated
1 tsp. lemon juice	¼ tsp. dry mustard
1 tsp. red wine vinegar	¼ tsp. dill weed
1 tsp. onion, minced	1 tsp. paprika

Preparation:
Steam till tender, about 10 minutes:
    cauliflower flowerets
Combine, blend in blender till smooth:
    cottage cheese
    1 tsp. lemon juice
    1 tsp. red wine vinegar
    1 tsp. minced onion
    2 Tbs. chopped parsley
    1 Tbs. grated Parmesan cheese
    ¼ tsp. dry mustard
    ¼ tsp. dill weed
Pour over cauliflower
Sprinkle with:
    1 tsp. paprika

Estimated nutrition information per serving:

Total fat	0.8 grams	Monounsaturated fat	0.2 grams
Saturated fat	0.4 grams	Polyunsaturated fat	0.1 grams
		Cholesterol	3 milligrams

TASTY CABBAGE
serves 4

Ingredients:

1 Tbs. water
3 cups cabbage, shredded
1 cup celery, chopped
1 cup red bell pepper, chopped

¾ cup onion, chopped
¼ tsp. salt
¼ tsp. savory
dash pepper

Preparation:

Heat in large skillet over medium heat:
1 Tbs. water

Combine and place in skillet:
chopped cabbage
chopped celery
chopped red bell pepper
chopped onion
¼ tsp. salt
¼ tsp. savory
dash pepper
Stir well
Cover, cook 5 minutes stirring occasionally
Serve immediately

Estimated nutrition information per serving:

Total fat	0 grams	Monounsaturated fat	0 grams
Saturated fat	0 grams	Polyunsaturated fat	0 grams
		Cholesterol	0 milligrams

SWEET & SOUR BROCCOLI
serves 5

Ingredients:

1 lb. broccoli flowerets
2 tsp. soft margarine
1 Tbs. brown sugar

3 Tbs. vinegar
⅛ tsp. dry mustard
¼ cup onion, chopped

Preparation:

Cook broccoli, drain
Combine in small saucepan:
    2 tsp. soft margarine
    1 Tbs. brown sugar
    3 Tbs. vinegar
    ⅛ tsp. dry mustard
    chopped onion
Heat till hot
Pour over cooked, drained broccoli
Serve immediately

Estimated nutrition information per serving:

Total fat	1.6 grams	Monounsaturated fat	0.5 grams
Saturated fat	0.3 grams	Polyunsaturated fat	0.7 grams
		Cholesterol	0 milligrams

PEAS, MUSHROOMS AND TOMATOES
serves 6

Ingredients:

1 medium onion, sliced
¾ tsp. ground turmeric
¼ tsp. ground ginger
1 10 oz. package frozen peas, thawed

½ lb. fresh whole mushrooms
2 tsp. fresh lemon juice
¼ tsp. salt
2 medium tomatoes, cut in wedges

Preparation:

Cook and stir in skillet over medium heat till onion tender:
sliced onion
¾ tsp. turmeric
¼ tsp. ginger
2 Tbs. water

Stir in:
peas
whole mushrooms
2 tsp. lemon juice
¼ tsp. salt
Cook uncovered, stirring occasionally till peas tender, about 3–5 minutes
Stir in tomato wedges
Heat just till hot

Estimated nutrition information per serving:

Total fat	0.2 grams	Monounsaturated fat	0.0 grams
Saturated fat	0.0 grams	Polyunsaturated fat	0.1 grams
		Cholesterol	0 milligrams

VEGETABLE STUFFED PEPPERS
serves 6

Ingredients:

6 medium green peppers
1½ cups corn
1 cup diced tomatoes
½ cup soft, whole grain bread
    crumbs
⅓ cup celery, finely chopped

1 tsp. Butter Buds
2 Tbs. minced onion
3 egg whites, slightly beaten
¼ tsp. salt
¼ tsp. basil, crushed
dash pepper

Preparation:

Remove tops and seeds from peppers

Combine in bowl:
    corn
    diced tomatoes
    bread crumbs
    chopped celery
    1 tsp. Butter Buds
    2 Tbs. minced onions
    slightly beaten egg whites
    ¼ tsp. salt
    ¼ tsp. basil
    dash pepper
Stuff peppers with mixture
Place peppers upright in greased baking dish

Add:
    small amount of water
Cover, bake at 350° for 1 hour

Estimated nutrition information per serving:

Total fat	0.5 grams	Monounsaturated fat	0.1 grams
Saturated fat	0.1 grams	Polyunsaturated fat	0.3 grams
		Cholesterol	0 milligrams

STUFFED POTATOES
serves 4

Ingredients:

2 large baking potatoes, scrubbed
¾ cup buttermilk
½ clove garlic
2 tsp. onion, minced

¼ tsp. pepper
¼ cup chives
¼ cup skim milk mozzarella cheese, shredded
paprika

Preparation:

Bake potatoes till tender
Remove potatoes from oven
Cut in half lengthwise
Scoop out pulp

Place in blender:
potato pulp
buttermilk
½ clove garlic
minced onion
¼ tsp. pepper
¼ cup chives
shredded cheese
Blend till fluffy and light
Spoon mixture back into potato shells
Sprinkle with paprika
Place potatoes under broiler till tops golden brown

Estimated nutrition information per serving:

Total fat	1.7 grams	Monounsaturated fat	0.5 grams
Saturated fat	1.1 grams	Polyunsaturated fat	0.1 grams
		Cholesterol	5 milligrams

"HOT" ZUCCHINI
serves 4–6

Ingredients:

2 Tbs. water or broth
1 lb. (4 cups) zucchini, sliced thin
1 cup carrots, shredded
1 large onion, chopped
¾ cup celery, chopped
½ medium green pepper, cut in
   thin strips
¼ tsp. salt
¼ tsp. garlic powder

½ tsp. dried basil, crushed
⅛ tsp. pepper
⅓ cup tomato sauce
¼ tsp. chili powder
1 tsp. vinegar
1 tsp. hot sauce
1 Tbs. prepared mustard
2 tomatoes, cut in wedges

Preparation:

Heat in large skillet:
   2 Tbs. water or broth

Add and mix together well:
   sliced zucchini
   shredded carrots
   chopped onion
   chopped celery
   pepper strips
   ¼ tsp. salt
   ¼ tsp. garlic powder
   ½ tsp. crushed basil
   ⅛ tsp. pepper
Cover, cook over med–high heat for 5 minutes, stir
   occasionally

Combine and stir into vegetables:
   tomato sauce
   ¼ tsp. chili powder
   1 tsp. vinegar
   1 tsp. hot sauce
   1 Tbs. prepared mustard
Add:
   tomato wedges
Cook uncovered 3–5 minutes or till thoroughly heated

Estimated nutrition information per serving:

Total fat	0.4 grams	Monounsaturated fat	0.0 grams
Saturated fat	0.1 grams	Polyunsaturated fat	0.2 grams
		Cholesterol	0 milligrams

VEGETABLE CASSEROLE
serves 6–8

Ingredients:

1 medium cauliflower head
1 eggplant
2 potatoes
1 Tbs. canola oil
1 tsp. mustard seed

1 tsp. curry powder
¼ tsp. salt
½ tsp. turmeric powder
1 cup peas
1 tomato, finely chopped
juice of 1 lemon

Preparation:

Remove:
    stem of cauliflower, cut into small pieces
Separate:
    flowerets, slice
Cut into ½" cubes:
    eggplant
Cube and boil till partially cooked:
    2 potatoes
Heat in Dutch oven:
    1 Tbs. canola oil
Add and brown, covered:
    1 tsp. mustard seed
Stir in:
    1 tsp. curry powder
    ¼ tsp. salt
    ½ tsp. turmeric powder
Add and stir to coat with spices and oil:
    cut cauliflower
Add:
    ¼ cup water
    cubed eggplant
    partially cooked potatoes
Continue cooking till almost desired doneness
Add 1 to 2 Tbs. water as needed, stirring gently
Add 5 minutes before serving:
    1 cup peas
When vegetables are cooked, stir in:
    chopped tomato
Turn off heat
Add lemon juice
Serve and enjoy

Estimated nutrition information per serving:

Total fat	1.9 grams	Monounsaturated fat	1.0 grams
Saturated fat	0.1 grams	Polyunsaturated fat	0.7 grams
		Cholesterol	0 milligrams

DRESSINGS AND DIPS

MOCK SOUR CREAM
1 cup

Ingredients:
1 cup nonfat plain yogurt
1 Tbs. chives, fresh or frozen

Preparation:
Mix yogurt and chives together
Serve with baked potatoes

Estimated nutrition information per serving, 1 Tbs.:

Total fat	0 grams	Monounsaturated fat	0.8 grams
Saturated fat	0 grams	Polyunsaturated fat	0.1 grams
		Cholesterol	1 milligram

or

Ingredients:
1 cup low fat cottage cheese
2 Tbs. skim buttermilk
1 tsp. lemon juice

Preparation:
Place into blender:
   cottage cheese
   buttermilk
   lemon juice
Blend till smooth

Estimated nutrition information per serving, 1 Tbs.:

Total fat	0.1 grams	Monounsaturated fat	0.0 grams
Saturated fat	0.1 grams	Polyunsaturated fat	0.1 grams
		Cholesterol	1 milligram

MAYONNAISE
1 cup

Ingredients:
2 Tbs. flour
⅔ cup skim milk
1 large egg, room temperature
½ tsp. dry mustard

¼ tsp. paprika
¼ tsp. salt
⅛ tsp. cayenne pepper
2 Tbs. fresh lemon juice
1 Tbs. olive oil

Preparation:
Put in jar and shake till mixed:
⅓ cup cold milk
2 Tbs. flour
Pour into top of double boiler over low heat and add:
⅓ cup milk
Mix together
Stir in:
egg
½ tsp. dry mustard
¼ tsp. paprika
¼ tsp. salt
⅛ tsp. cayenne pepper
Cook over just simmering water, stirring constantly till thickened and smooth
Remove from heat and stir in:
2 Tbs. lemon juice
1 Tbs. olive oil
Cool and refrigerate in tightly covered container

Estimated nutrition information per serving, 1 Tbs.:

Total fat	1.3 grams	Monounsaturated fat	0.8 grams
Saturated fat	0.2 grams	Polyunsaturated fat	0.1 grams
		Cholesterol	17 milligrams

DILL AND YOGURT DRESSING
1 cup

Ingredients:

1 cup plain low fat yogurt	2 tsp. finely chopped fresh parsley
½ tsp. dill weed, crushed	¼ tsp. dry mustard
2 tsp. onion, minced	⅛ tsp. garlic powder
1 tsp. lemon juice	

Preparation:
Combine in small bowl:
All above ingredients
Cover, refrigerate for several hours to blend flavors

Estimated nutrition information per serving, 2 Tbs.:

Total fat	0.5 grams	Monounsaturated fat	0.1 grams
Saturated fat	0.3 grams	Polyunsaturated fat	0 grams
		Cholesterol	2 milligrams

RUSSIAN SOUR CREAM DRESSING
about 2 cups

Ingredients:

3 hard boiled egg whites, chopped
1 cup low fat (1%) yogurt
2 Tbs. lemon juice

1 Tbs. drained capers
2 gherkin pickles, minced
salt
pepper

Preparation:

Mix all above ingredients together
Refrigerate at least 1 hour before using

Estimated nutrition information per serving, 1 Tbs.:

Total fat	0.1 grams	Monounsaturated fat	0 grams
Saturated fat	0.1 grams	Polyunsaturated fat	0 grams
		Cholesterol	0 milligrams

CHILI BEAN DIP
about 1⅓ cup

Ingredients:

15 oz. can kidney beans
3 Tbs. bean liquid
1 Tbs. vinegar
1 tsp. chili powder

⅛ tsp. ground cumin
2 tsp. onion, grated
2 tsp. parsley, chopped

Preparation:

Drain:
   kidney beans, reserve liquid
Place in blender:
   beans
   3 Tbs. bean liquid
   1 Tbs. vinegar
   1 tsp. chili powder
   ⅛ tsp. ground cumin
Blend till smooth
Remove from blender and stir in:
   2 tsp. grated onion
   2 tsp. chopped parsley
Chill thoroughly
Serve with raw vegetable sticks

Estimated nutrition information per serving, 1 Tbs.:

Total fat	0.2 grams	Monounsaturated fat	0 grams
Saturated fat	0 grams	Polyunsaturated fat	0.1 grams
		Cholesterol	0 milligrams

DESSERTS

Dessert is the end of the meal pleasure that should be eaten in a small quantity and savored. For low fat content, fruits, gelatins, puddings, and sherbet are at the top of the list. Be careful of cookies, cakes, cobblers and pies with pies having the highest fat content because of the fat in the crust.

APPLE COOKIES
about 5 dozen small

Ingredients:

1 cup whole wheat pastry flour
¾ cup oat bran
½ tsp. salt
¾ tsp. baking powder
½ tsp. baking soda
¾ tsp. cinnamon
½ tsp. ground cloves
½ tsp. cardamon (optional)

½ cup walnuts, chopped
¼ cup concentrated pineapple juice
⅓ cup light olive oil
4 egg whites
1 cup rolled oats
2 large apples, chopped
½ cup raisins
½ cup dried apricots, chopped

Preparation:

Stir together in small bowl:
  whole wheat flour
  oat bran
  ½ tsp. salt
  ¾ tsp. baking powder
  ½ tsp. baking soda
  ¾ tsp. cinnamon
  ½ tsp. cloves
  ½ tsp. cardamon (optional)
  ½ cup chopped walnuts
Beat together in large bowl:
  ¼ cup concentrated pineapple juice
  ⅓ cup light olive oil
Beat in:
  4 egg whites
Stir in:
  flour mixture
  rolled oats
  2 chopped apples
  ½ cup raisins
  ½ cup chopped apricots
Mix well

Drop by teaspoon, 2″ apart onto cookie sheet sprayed with
  nonstick oil
Bake at 350° 12–15 minutes
And hide!

Estimated nutrition information per cookie:

Total fat	2.0 grams	Monounsaturated fat	1.1 grams
Saturated fat	0.2 grams	Polyunsaturated fat	0.6 grams
		Cholesterol	0 milligrams

RAISIN OATMEAL COOKIES
4 dozen

Ingredients:

1½ cups whole wheat pastry flour
½ cup oat bran
1 tsp. baking soda
½ tsp. salt
1 tsp. cinnamon
¼ + ⅛ tsp. cloves
¼ + ⅛ tsp. nutmeg
3 cups rolled oats

4 egg whites, slightly beaten
¼ cup concentrated pineapple juice
½ cup apples, chopped
½ cup canola oil
½ cup skim milk
½ cup orange juice
2 tsp. vanilla
2 cup raisins

Preparation:

Stir together with fork in bowl:
flour
oat bran
1 tsp. baking soda
½ tsp. salt
1 tsp. cinnamon
¼ + ⅛ tsp. cloves
¼ + ⅛ tsp. nutmeg
rolled oats

Combine in small bowl:
beaten egg whites
¼ cup concentrated pineapple juice
½ cup chopped apples
½ cup canola oil
½ cup skim milk
½ cup orange juice
2 tsp. vanilla
raisins

Add to flour mixture
Mix well
Place teaspoons of batter on slightly oiled cookie sheet
Bake at 375° 12–15 minutes
Bake shorter time for chewy cookie and longer for crisp cookie

Estimated nutrition information per cookie:

Total fat	2.5 grams	Monounsaturated fat	1.3 grams
Saturated fat	0.2 grams	Polyunsaturated fat	0.8 grams
		Cholesterol	0 milligrams

CHOCOLATE COOKIES
3 dozen cookies

Ingredients:
⅓ cup + 1 Tbs. canola oil
⅓ cup + 2 Tbs. sugar
2 egg whites, beaten
6 Tbs. cocoa
1¾ cups minus 1 Tbs. whole wheat pastry flour

2¼ tsp. baking powder
¼ tsp. salt
½ cup skim milk
1½ tsp. vanilla

Preparation:
Cream together in small bowl:
  ⅓ cup + 1 Tbs. canola oil
  ⅓ cup + 2 Tbs. sugar
Beat in:
  egg whites
Combine:
  6 Tbs. cocoa
  flour
  2¼ tsp. baking powder
  ¼ tsp. salt

Add egg mixture to dry mixture alternately with:
  ½ cup milk
Mix well, stir in:
  1½ tsp. vanilla
Using teaspoon, drop batter 2" apart onto lightly oiled cookie sheet
Bake at 400° for 8 to 10 minutes

Estimated nutrition information per cookie:

Total fat	2.5 grams	Monounsaturated fat	1.3 grams
Saturated fat	0.2 grams	Polyunsaturated fat	0.9 grams
		Cholesterol	0 milligrams

ANGEL FOOD CAKE
serves 12

Ingredients:
1 cup sifted flour
½ cup superfine sugar
1½ tsp. cream of tartar

1½ cups (12) egg whites
2 tsp. vanilla
¼ tsp. salt

Preparation:
    Sift together 4 times:
      flour
      ¼ cup sugar
    Beat till stiff enough to hold soft peaks:
      egg whites
      1½ tsp. cream of tartar
      ¼ tsp. salt
      2 tsp. vanilla
    Add 1 Tbs. at a time, beat after each addition:
      ¼ cup sugar
    Sift over egg whites:
      flour mixture, ¼ cup at a time and fold in after each addition
    Push batter into 10″ clean, ungreased tube pan
    Gently cut with knife through batter in ever-widening circles
      to break air bubbles
    Bake at 375° for 35–40 minutes
    Remove from oven, invert pan till cake cool
    Remove from pan

Estimated nutrition information per serving:

Total fat	trace grams	Monounsaturated fat	0 grams
Saturated fat	0 grams	Polyunsaturated fat	0 grams
		Cholesterol	0 milligrams

SOFT STRAWBERRY ICE CREAM
serves 4

Ingredients:
    2 cups 1% milk
    2 cups frozen strawberries
    1½ tsp. vanilla
    2 Tbs. concentrated pineapple juice
    ½ cup non-instant dry low fat milk
      powder

Preparation:
    Blend above ingredients in blender till thick and smooth
    Serve immediately for soft ice cream
      or
    Freeze in ice cube trays, stirring once before freezing com-
      pleted

Estimated nutrition information per serving:

Total fat	1.1 grams	Monounsaturated fat	0.4 grams
Saturated fat	0.8 grams	Polyunsaturated fat	0.2 grams
		Cholesterol	7 milligrams

FRUIT SHERBET
serves 4

Ingredients:
1 cup plain nonfat yogurt
1 Tbs. concentrated orange juice
½ cup orange juice
2 cups fresh or frozen strawberries

1 lb. can crushed pineapple in own juice
½ cup non-instant milk powder
1 banana, cut in chunks
1 Tbs. lemon juice

Preparation:
Blend together till smooth:
    all above ingredients
Freeze in ice cube trays or other container
Beat once before freezing completed

Estimated nutrition information per serving:

Total fat	0.4 grams	Monounsaturated fat	0.0 grams
Saturated fat	0.2 grams	Polyunsaturated fat	0.0 grams
		Cholesterol	3 milligrams

WHIPPED CREAM
3 cups

Ingredients:
12 oz can evaporated skimmed milk
2 Tbs. + 1½ tsp. lemon juice

1 Tbs. vanilla
1 Tbs. sugar

Preparation:
Chill milk thoroughly in can
Pour cold milk into cold bowl
Whip with cold beaters
When milk very stiff, beat in:
    2 Tbs. + 1½ tsp. lemon juice (insures stiffness)
    1 Tbs. vanilla
    1 Tbs. sugar
Refrigerate till ready to use

Estimated nutrition information per ¼ cup:

Total fat	0.1 grams	Monounsaturated fat	0.0 grams
Saturated fat	0.1 grams	Polyunsaturated fat	0.0 grams
		Cholesterol	1 milligrams

PINEAPPLE CREAM
serves 6

Ingredients:

3¼ cups unsweetened pineapple jc.
2 envelopes unflavored gelatin
1 cup unsweetened crushed
   pineapple, drained
1 banana, thinly sliced

½ cup cold evaporated skim milk
½ tsp vanilla
1 Tbs. concentrate pineapple juice
1½ tsp. lemon juice

Preparation:

Pour into small saucepan:
   ½ cup unsweetened pineapple juice
Sprinkle on juice:
   2 envelopes gelatin
Heat over medium heat, stirring constantly till gelatin
   dissolves
Pour into bowl with:
   2¾ cups unsweetened pineapple juice
Stir well

Chill till mixture partially set
Beat gelatin mixture till frothy

Add:
   1 cup crushed pineapple, drained
   1 sliced banana
Beat till peaks form:
   ½ cup chilled evaporated milk

Add:
   ½ tsp. vanilla
   1 Tbs. concentrated pineapple juice
   1½ tsp. lemon juice
Fold into gelatin
Place in sherbet glasses or 5 cup mold

Estimated nutrition information per serving:

Total fat	0.3 grams	Monounsaturated fat	0.0 grams
Saturated fat	0.1 grams	Polyunsaturated fat	0.0 grams
		Cholesterol	1 milligrams

APPLE RASPBERRY WITH PEACHES
serves 6–8

Ingredients:
    2 envelopes plain gelatin
    ½ cup cold water
    3 cups Apple Raspberry juice
    2 large fresh peaches, sliced
    1 cup fresh Bing cherries, pitted
       and cut in half

Preparation:
Sprinkle:
    2 envelopes gelatin
On:
    ½ cup cold water in small saucepan
Heat, stirring constantly, until gelatin dissolves completely
Add to:
    3 cups Apple Raspberry juice
Mix well
Place in refrigerator till slightly set
Fold in:
    sliced peaches
    halved Bing cherries
Return to refrigerator till firm
May be served with plain nonfat yogurt as topping

Estimated nutrition information per serving:
Total fat	0.0 grams	Monounsaturated fat	0.0 grams
Saturated fat	0.0 grams	Polyunsaturated fat	0.0 grams
		Cholesterol	0 milligrams

ORANGE PINEAPPLE GELATIN
serves 6–8

Ingredients:
    2 envelopes plain gelatin
    ½ cup cold water
    1¾ cups orange juice

    1½ cups unsweetened pineapple
       juice
    2 oranges cut in small pieces
    1 banana, sliced

Preparation:
Pour into small saucepan:
    ½ cup cold water

Sprinkle over water:
   2 envelopes gelatin
Heat, stirring constantly till gelatin dissolved

Add:
   1¾ cups orange juice
   1½ cups pineapple juice
Mix thoroughly
Pour into bowl
Place in refrigerator till slightly set

Fold in:
   orange pieces
   banana slices
Return to refrigerator till firm

Estimated nutrition information per serving, ⅛:
Total fat	0.0 grams	Monounsaturated fat 0.0 grams
Saturated fat	0.0 grams	Polyunsaturated fat 0.0 grams
		Cholesterol 0 milligrams

BANANA & YOGURT
serves 4

Ingredients:

⅛ tsp. cinnamon
2 Tbs. concentrated pineapple juice
1 tsp. vanilla
½ cup plain nonfat yogurt
⅛ tsp. nutmeg
4 medium bananas, sliced

Preparation:
Mix together in bowl:
   ⅛ tsp. cinnamon
   2 Tbs. concentrated juice
   1 tsp. vanilla
   ½ cup yogurt
   ⅛ tsp. nutmeg
Fold in:
   sliced bananas
Chill
Serve topped with sliced fresh fruit if desired

Estimated nutrition information per serving:
Total fat	1.5 grams	Monounsaturated fat 0.1 grams
Saturated fat	0.5 grams	Polyunsaturated fat 0.1 grams
		Cholesterol 2 milligrams

OAT BRAN PIE CRUST
1 9″ crust

Ingredients:
1 cup whole wheat pastry flour
½ cup oat bran
¼ tsp. salt
¼ cup canola oil
3 Tbs. ice water

Preparation:
Combine:
   1 cup flour
   ½ cup oat bran
   ¼ tsp. salt
Stir in:
   ¼ cup oil

Add while crumbling with hands:
   3 Tbs. ice water
Form into ball
Roll out between 2 sheets of waxed paper
Place in lightly oiled pie plate
Prick with fork

Bake at 425° for 12–15 minutes if baked pie crust needed

Estimated nutrition information per serving, ⅙ of crust:

Total fat	10.3 grams	Monounsaturated fat	5.9 grams
Saturated fat	0.6 grams	Polyunsaturated fat	3.4 grams
		Cholesterol	0 milligrams

LEMON MERINGUE PIE
1 9" pie

Ingredients:

1 baked oat bran pie crust
½ cup + 2 Tbs. sugar
3 Tbs. cornstarch
1 lemon rind grated
¼ cup + 2 tsp. fresh lemon juice

1 Tbs. soft margarine
1 egg + 2 egg whites slightly
   beaten
1½ cups boiling water
3 egg whites, room temperature
⅛ tsp. cream tartar

Preparation:

Mix in top of double boiler:
   ½ cup sugar
   3 Tbs. cornstarch

Add and mix well:
   grated lemon rind
   lemon juice
   margarine
   slightly beaten eggs

Add very slowly while stirring constantly:
   boiling water
Cook over hot water while stirring, till thick
Cool

Beat till almost stiff:
   3 egg whites
   ⅛ tsp. cream of tartar
Continue to beat till stiff while slowly adding:
   2 Tbs. sugar
Pour cooled filling into baked pie crust
Spread meringue entirely over filling, touching crust

Bake at 300° for 20–30 minutes

Estimated nutrition information per serving, ⅙ of pie:

Total fat	13.1 grams	Monounsaturated fat	6.9 grams
Saturated fat	0.9 grams	Polyunsaturated fat	4.3 grams
		Cholesterol	35 milligrams

GOOD OLD RICE PUDDING
serves 6

Ingredients:

4 cups 1% milk	¼ tsp. salt
¼ cup brown rice	¼ cup raisins
2 Tbs. sugar	¼ tsp. nutmeg

Preparation:

Combine in bowl:
   4 cups milk
   ¼ cup rice
   2 Tbs. sugar
   ¼ tsp. salt
Pour into lightly oiled 1½ quart baking dish
Bake at 300° for 1 hour, stir frequently (every 15–20 minutes)
Stir in:
   ¼ cup raisins
   ¼ tsp. nutmeg
Continue baking 1½ hours
Remove from oven, place on rack to cool

May be served warm or cold
When first removed from oven, may seem runny, but by time
   it has cooled, the milk will have either thickened or become
   absorbed.

Estimated nutrition information per serving:

Total fat	1.5 grams	Monounsaturated fat	0.5 grams
Saturated fat	1.0 grams	Polyunsaturated fat	0.1 grams
		Cholesterol	7 milligrams

BREADS

Muffins will spoil quickly in warm weather. May refrigerate or freeze. Reheat in microwave or toaster oven.

MOLASSES BRAN BREAD
serves 12

Ingredients:
1 tsp. baking soda
2 Tbs. molasses
2 Tbs. concentrated apple juice
1½ cups buttermilk

1½ cups whole wheat flour
1½ cups oat bran
⅓ cup raisins

Preparation:
Dissolve in bowl by stirring:
  1 tsp. baking soda
In:
  2 Tbs. molasses
Add:
  2 Tbs. apple juice
  1½ cups buttermilk
  1½ cups flour
  1½ cups bran
  ⅓ cup raisins
Mix till completely mixed
Pour into loaf pan

Bake at 350° for 45 minutes

Estimated nutrition information per serving:

Total fat	1.4 grams	Monounsaturated fat	0.9 grams
Saturated fat	0.2 grams	Polyunsaturated fat	0.2 grams
		Cholesterol	1 milligram

BISCUITS
10–12

Ingredients:
2 cups whole wheat pastry flour
4 tsp. baking powder
¼ tsp. salt

¾ cup skim milk
3 Tbs. canola oil

Preparation:
Combine:
  flour
  4 tsp. baking powder
  ¼ tsp. salt
Combine and add:
  ¾ cup milk
  3 Tbs. canola oil

Stir enough to hold dough together
Turn out onto well floured area
Knead lightly, about 10 times
Pat or roll dough to ½" thick
Cut with floured cutter
Place on ungreased baking sheet

Bake at 425° for 10–12 minutes

Estimated nutrition information per serving:

Total fat	4.0 grams	Monounsaturated fat	2.1 grams
Saturated fat	0.3 grams	Polyunsaturated fat	1.4 grams
		Cholesterol	0 milligrams

NO OIL MUFFINS
12 muffins

Ingredients:

2¼ cups oat bran
1 Tbs. baking powder
1 Tbs. brown sugar
¼ cup raisins
¼ cup dried apricots, chopped

1 cup nonfat milk
½ cup orange juice
2 egg whites
2 Tbs. corn syrup

Preparation:

Combine in medium bowl:
   oat bran
   1 Tbs. baking powder
   1 Tbs. brown sugar
   ¼ cup raisins
   ¼ cup chopped apricots
Mix in small bowl:
   1 cup milk
   ½ cup orange juice
   egg whites
   2 Tbs. corn syrup
Blend with dry ingredients
Pour into paper baking cup lined muffin tins
Bake at 425° for 13–15 minutes or till inserted pick comes out
   clean
Remove from pan and serve immediately if desired

Estimated nutrition information per serving:

Total fat	1.3 grams	Monounsaturated fat	0.8 grams
Saturated fat	0.08 grams	Polyunsaturated fat	0.4 grams
		Cholesterol	.5 milligrams

CORN MUFFINS
10–12 muffins

Ingredients:

⅓ cup stirred whole wheat flour
1 tsp. baking powder
¼ tsp. salt
½ tsp. baking soda
1 Tbs. sugar

1⅓ cups yellow corn meal
1 egg or 2 egg whites, beaten
1 cup lowfat plain yogurt
2 Tbs. canola oil

Preparation:

Stir together in bowl:
  flour
  1 tsp. baking powder
  ¼ tsp. salt
  ½ tsp. baking soda
  1 Tbs. sugar
  corn meal

Beat together in small bowl:
  egg
  yogurt
  2 Tbs. canola oil

Make a well in dry ingredients
Add yogurt mixture
Stir till just blended
Pour into oiled muffin tins

Bake at 400° for 25 minutes

Estimated nutrition information per serving: (made with 1 whole egg)

Total fat	3.4 grams	Monounsaturated fat 1.7 grams
Saturated fat	0.5 grams	Polyunsaturated fat 1.0 grams
		Cholesterol 20 milligrams

APPLE AND NUT BUNS
serves 12

Ingredients:

Buns	Filling
2½ cup stirred whole wheat flour	1 Tbs. soft margarine, melted
4¼ tsp. baking powder	3 apples, diced
¼ tsp. salt	½ cup almonds, coarsely chopped
3 Tbs. canola oil	¼ cup raisins
¾ cup nonfat milk	1 Tbs. sugar
	½ tsp. cinnamon
	2 Tbs. molasses

Preparation:
Buns
  Sift together:
      2½ cups stirred flour
      4¼ tsp. baking powder
      ¼ tsp salt
  Combine:
      3 Tbs. canola oil
      ¾ cup milk
  Add gradually to flour mixture, stirring constantly
  Turn onto floured board and knead 30 seconds
  Roll out to ½" thick
Filling
  Spread on dough:
      melted margarine
  Sprinkle on:
      diced apples
      chopped nuts
      raisins
      1 Tbs. sugar
      ½ tsp. cinnamon
  Dribble over filling:
      1 Tbs. molasses
  Roll up as for jelly roll
  Cut in 1" slices
  Place in lightly oiled pan about 1" apart
  Dribble over buns:
      1 Tbs. molasses
  Bake at 400 degrees for 20 minutes

Estimated nutrition information per serving:

Total fat	7.9 grams	Monounsaturated fat	4.4 grams
Saturated fat	0.8 grams	Polyunsaturated fat	2.5 grams
		Cholesterol	0 milligrams

SOLUBLE FIBER[1] CONTENT OF VARIOUS FOODS

Food Item 3½ oz. (100 Grams)	Soluble Fiber Grams	Food Item 3½ oz. (100 Grams)	Soluble Fiber Grams
Cereals		**Vegetables** *continued*	
All-Bran	0.0	Corn	1.1
Benefit	10.0	Cucumbers	0.9
Bran Buds	0.9	Eggplant	0.9
Cornflakes	3.4	Green peppers	0.0
Cracked wheat	0.4	Kale, cooked	0.8
Farina	0.1	Lettuce	0.6
Grape-Nuts	0.2	Mushrooms	0.9
Grits	3.3	Onions, raw	1.0
Oat bran	9.2	Onions, cooked	0.8
Rolled oats	3.0	Parsnips	0.5
Rice bran	7.0	Peas, cooked	2.4
Shredded wheat	0.4	Potatoes, sweet, cooked	2.2
Wheat flakes	0.4	Potatoes, white, cooked	2.0
		Radishes	0.5
Flours & Breads		Rice, brown, cooked	0.0
Rye flour, light	0.3	Rice, white, cooked	0.0
Rye flour, dark	0.4	Spaghetti	0.1
White flour	0.1	Spinach	1.4
Whole wheat flour	0.3	Squash, summer, raw	1.4
Graham crackers, plain	0.3	Squash, summer, cooked	1.0
Rye crackers	0.3	Squash, winter, cooked	0.3
Saltine crackers	0.1	Tomatoes, raw	0.4
Corn muffin	0.9	Tomatoes, cooked	0.3
Oat bran muffin	3.0	Turnips	1.0
Whole wheat muffin	0.1	Zucchini	1.4
Corn bread	1.1		
French bread	0.1	**Fruits**	
Rye bread	0.3	Apple	2.0
White bread	0.1	Applesauce	0.8
Whole wheat bread	0.3	Apple juice	0.1
		Apricots	1.0
Vegetables		Apricots, canned	0.8
Asparagus, raw	0.5	Banana	0.9
Asparagus, cooked	0.4	Blackberries	0.9
Barley, dry	0.4	Cherries	0.4
Beans, green; cooked	0.8	Cranberry juice	0.0
Beans, kidney; cooked	0.5	Grapes	0.2
Beans, lima	0.4	Grape juice	0.0
Beans, pinto	1.0	Grapefruit	0.9
Bean sprouts, mung	0.6	Lemon juice	0.0
Beans, white; cooked	0.5	Muskmelon	0.3
Beet, cooked	0.9	Orange	0.6
Broccoli	2.1	Orange juice	0.3
Brussels sprouts, cooked	0.9	Peach	0.7
Cabbage, raw	1.7	Peaches, canned	1.6
Cabbage, cooked	1.4	Pear	0.6
Carrots, raw	2.5	Pears, canne	0.3
Carrots, cooked	1.4	Pineapple	0.3
Cauliflower, raw	0.5	Plum	1.0
Cauliflower, cooked	0.3	Strawberries	0.8
Celery, raw	0.8	Tangerine	1.6
Celery, cooked	0.6		

[1] Meat, milk and milk products contain no soluble fiber.

NUTRITIVE VALUE
OF FOODS TABLE*

Calorie, Protein, Carbohydrate, Fat
and Cholesterol Content of Various Foods

FOODS ARE GROUPED
UNDER THE FOLLOWING MAIN HEADINGS

Beverages

Dairy Products

Eggs

Fats & Oils

Fish & Shellfish

Fruit & Fruit Juices

Grain Products

Legumes, Nuts & Seeds

Meat & Meat Products

Mixed Dishes & Fast Foods

Poultry & Poultry Products

Soups, Sauces & Gravies

Sugar & Sweets

Vegetable & Vegetable Products

Miscellaneous

The use of the table can be a very valuable tool in helping you understand what you eat. The information affords you an understanding of the chemistry of various foods. By knowing their chemistry, you have a better opportunity to select foods more suited to your present and long term needs for improved health.

*Data from the United States Department of Agriculture, Human Nutrition Information Service; Home and Garden Bulletin Number 72

Foods	Approximate Measure (Portion)	Weight (Grams)	Calories (Calories)	Protein (Grams)	Carbohydrate (Grams)	Total Fat (Grams)	Fats Saturated (Grams)	Fats Mono-unsaturated (Grams)	Fats Poly-unsaturated (Grams)	Cholesterol (Milligrams)
Beverages										
Alcoholic										
Beer										
Regular	12 oz	360	150	1	13	0	0	0	0	0
Light	12 oz	355	95	1	5	0	0	0	0	0
Gin, rum, vodka, whiskey										
80-proof	1½ oz	42	95	0	tr	0	0	0	0	0
86-proof	1½ oz	42	105	0	tr	0	0	0	0	0
90-proof	1½ oz	42	110	0	tr	0	0	0	0	0
Wines										
Dessert	3½ oz	103	140	tr	8	0	0	0	0	0
Table										
Red	3½ oz	102	75	tr	3	0	0	0	0	0
White	3½ oz	102	80	tr	3	0	0	0	0	0
Carbonated										
Club soda	1 oz	30	0	0	0	0	0	0	0	0
Cola type										
Regular	1 oz	30	13	0	3	0	0	0	0	0
Diet	1 oz	30	tr	0	tr	0	0	0	0	0
Ginger ale	1 oz	30	10	0	3	0	0	0	0	0
Grape	1 oz	30	15	0	4	0	0	0	0	0
Lemon-lime	1 oz	30	13	0	3	0	0	0	0	0
Orange	1 oz	30	15	0	4	0	0	0	0	0
Pepper type	1 oz	30	13	0	3	0	0	0	0	0
Root beer	1 oz	30	13	0	3	0	0	0	0	0

Cocoa & chocolate-flavored
  See dairy products
Coffee
  Brewed ....6 oz
  Instant, 2 tsp. powder
    in 6 oz. water ....6 oz
Fruit drinks
  Canned
    Fruit punch drink.......6 oz
    Grape drink............6 oz
    Pineapple-grapefruit juice drink....6 oz
  Frozen
    Lemonade concentrate
      Undiluted..............6 oz
      Diluted with 4⅓ parts water
        by volume ....6 oz
    Limeade concentrate
      Undiluted..............6 oz
      Diluted with 4⅓ parts water
        by volume ....6 oz
Fruit juices, see under fruits
Milk beverages, see dairy products
Tea
  Brewed ....8 oz
  Instant, powder
    Unsweetened, 1 tsp. powder
      + 8 oz water............8 oz
    Sweetened, 3 tsp. powder
      + 8 oz water............8 oz

Item	Measure								
Brewed	6 oz	180	tr	tr	tr	tr	tr	tr	tr	0
Instant, 2 tsp. powder in 6 oz. water	6 oz	182	tr	tr	1	tr	tr	tr	tr	0
Fruit punch drink	6 oz	190	85	tr	22	0	0	0	0	0
Grape drink	6 oz	187	100	tr	26	0	0	0	0	0
Pineapple-grapefruit juice drink	6 oz	187	90	tr	23	tr	tr	tr	tr	0
Lemonade, Undiluted	6 oz	219	425	tr	112	tr	tr	tr	tr	0
Lemonade, Diluted with 4⅓ parts water by volume	6 oz	185	80	tr	21	tr	tr	tr	tr	0
Limeade, Undiluted	6 oz	218	410	tr	108	tr	tr	tr	tr	0
Limeade, Diluted with 4⅓ parts water by volume	6 oz	185	75	tr	20	tr	tr	tr	tr	0
Tea, Brewed	8 oz	240	tr	tr	tr	tr	tr	tr	tr	0
Tea, Unsweetened, 1 tsp. powder + 8 oz water	8 oz	241	tr	tr	1	tr	tr	tr	tr	0
Tea, Sweetened, 3 tsp. powder + 8 oz water	8 oz	262	85	tr	22	tr	tr	tr	tr	0

(tr indicates nutrient present in trace amount)

191

Foods	Approximate Measure	Weight	Calories	Protein	Carbohydrate	Total Fat	Fats			Cholesterol
							Saturated	Mono-unsaturated	Poly-unsaturated	
	Portion	Grams	Calories	Grams	Grams	Grams	Grams	Grams	Grams	Milligrams
Dairy Products										
Butter..................	½ cup	113	810	1	tr	92	57	26	3.4	247
	1 Tbs	14	100	tr	tr	11	7.1	3.3	0.4	31
	1 pat	5	35	tr	tr	4	2.5	1.2	0.2	11
Cheese										
Natural										
Blue..............1 oz	28	100	6	1	8	5.3	2.2	0.2	21	
Camembert..........1.33 oz	38	115	8	tr	9	5.8	2.7	0.3	27	
Cheddar.............1 oz	28	115	7	tr	9	6.0	2.7	0.3	30	
Cube...............1 in	17	70	4	tr	6	3.6	1.6	0.2	18	
Shredded...........1 cup	113	455	28	1	37	23.8	10.6	1.1	119	
Cottage (curd not pressed down)										
Creamed (cottage cheese, 4% fat)										
Large curd ....1 cup	225	235	28	6	10	6.4	2.9	0.3	34	
Small curd ....1 cup	210	215	26	6	9	6.0	2.7	0.3	31	
With fruit ....1 cup	226	280	22	30	8	4.9	2.2	0.2	108	
Lowfat (2%) ....1 cup	226	205	31	8	4	2.8	1.2	0.1	19	
Uncreamed (cottage cheese dry curd, less than ½% fat) ....1 cup	145	125	25	3	1	0.4	0.2	tr	10	
Cream................1 oz	28	100	2	1	10	6.2	2.8	0.4	31	
Feta ....1 oz	28	75	4	1	6	4.2	1.3	0.2	25	
Mozzarella, made with:										
Whole milk...........1 oz	28	80	6	1	6	3.7	1.9	0.2	22	
Part skim milk........1 oz	28	80	8	1	5	3.1	1.4	0.1	15	
Muenster ....1 oz	28	105	7	tr	9	5.4	2.5	0.2	27	

Food	Measure									
Parmesan, grated:										
Not pressed down	1 cup	100	455	42	4	30	19.1	8.7	0.7	79
	1 Tbs	5	25	tr	2	1	1.0	0.4	tr	4
Provolone	1 oz	28	130	12	1	9	5.4	2.5	0.2	22
Ricotta, made with:	1 oz	28	100	7	1	8	4.8	2.1	0.2	20
Whole milk	1 cup	246	430	28	7	32	20.4	8.9	0.9	124
Part skim milk	1 cup	246	340	28	13	19	12.1	5.7	0.6	76
Swiss	1 oz	28	105	8	1	8	5.0	2.1	0.3	26
Pasteurized process:										
American	1 oz	28	105	6	tr	9	5.6	2.5	0.3	27
Swiss	1 oz	28	95	7	1	7	4.5	2.0	0.2	24
Pasteurized process cheese food, American	1 oz	28	95	6	2	7	4.4	2.0	0.2	18
Pasteurized process cheese spread, American	1 oz	28	80	5	2	6	3.8	1.8	0.2	16
Cream, sweet:										
Half & Half	1 cup	242	315	7	10	28	17.3	8.0	1.0	89
	1 Tbs	15	20	tr	1	2	1.1	0.5	0.1	6
Light	1 cup	240	470	6	9	46	28.8	13.4	1.7	159
	1 Tbs	15	30	tr	1	3	1.8	0.8	0.1	10
Whipping, unwhipped:										
Light	1 cup	239	700	5	7	74	46.2	21.7	2.1	265
	1 Tbs	15	45	tr	tr	5	2.9	1.4	0.1	17
Heavy	1 cup	238	820	5	7	88	54.8	25.4	3.3	326
	1 Tbs	15	50	tr	tr	6	3.5	1.6	0.2	21
Whipped topping (pressurized)	1 cup	60	155	2	7	13	8.3	3.9	0.5	46
	1 Tbs	3	10	tr	tr	1	0.4	0.2	tr	2
Cream, sour	1 cup	230	495	7	10	48	30.0	13.9	1.8	102
	1 Tbs	12	25	tr	1	3	1.6	0.7	0.1	5

Dairy Products continued

| Foods | Approximate Measure | Weight | Calories | Protein | Carbohydrate | Total Fat | Fats | | | Cholesterol |
| | Portion | Grams | Calories | Grams | Grams | Grams | Saturated | Mono-unsaturated | Poly-unsaturated | Milligrams |
							Grams	Grams	Grams	
Cream products, imitation (made with vegetable fat):										
Sweet:										
Creamers:										
Liquid (frozen) ....1 Tbs	15	20	tr	2	1	1.4	tr	tr	0
Powdered.................1 tsp	2	10	tr	1	1	0.7	tr	tr	0
Whipped topping:										
Frozen.....................1 cup	75	240	1	17	19	16.3	1.2	0.4	0
1 Tbs	4	15	tr	1	1	0.9	0.1	tr	0
Powdered, made with										
whole milk................1 cup	80	150	3	13	10	8.5	0.7	0.2	8
1 Tbs	4	10	tr	1	tr	0.4	tr	tr	tr
Pressurized................1 cup	70	185	1	11	16	13.2	1.3	0.2	0
1 Tbs	4	10	tr	1	1	0.8	0.1	tr	0
Sour dressing (filled cream type product, nonbutterfat).........1 cup	235	415	8	11	39	31.2	4.6	1.1	13
1 Tbs	12	20	tr	1	2	1.6	0.2	0.1	1
Ice cream, vanilla:										
Regular (11% fat):										
Hardened....................1 cup	133	270	5	32	14	8.9	4.1	0.5	59
3 oz	50	100	2	12	5	3.4	1.6	0.2	22
Soft serve (frozen custard) ....1 cup	173	375	7	38	23	13.5	6.7	1.0	153
Rich (16% fat), hardened ....1 cup	148	350	4	32	24	4.7	6.8	0.9	88

194

Food	Measure	Grams	(col)	(col)	(col)	(col)	(col)	(col)	(col)	(col)
Ice milk, vanilla:										
Hardened (4% fat)	1 cup	131	5	185	29	6	3.5	1.6	0.2	18
Soft serve (3% fat)	1 cup	175	8	225	38	5	2.9	1.3	0.2	13
Sherbet (2% fat)	1 cup	193	2	270	59	4	2.4	1.1	0.1	14
Milk										
Fluid:										
Whole (3.3% fat)	1 cup	244	8	150	11	8	5.1	2.4	0.3	33
Lowfat (2%):										
No milk solids added	1 cup	244	8	120	12	5	2.9	1.4	0.2	18
Milk solids added, label claim										
<10 g protein per cup	1 cup	245	9	125	12	5	2.9	1.4	0.2	18
Lowfat (1%):										
No milk solids added	1 cup	244	8	100	12	3	1.6	0.7	0.1	10
Milk solids added, label claim										
<10 g protein per cup	1 cup	245	9	105	12	2	1.5	0.7	0.1	10
Nonfat (skim):										
No milk solids added	1 cup	245	8	85	12	tr	0.3	0.1	tr	4
Milk solids added, label claim										
<10 g protein per cup	1 cup	245	9	90	12	1	0.4	0.2	tr	5
Buttermilk	1 cup	245	8	100	12	2	1.3	0.6	0.1	9
Canned:										
Condensed, sweet	1 cup	306	24	980	166	27	16.8	7.4	1.0	104
Evaporated:										
Whole milk	1 cup	252	17	340	25	19	11.6	5.9	0.6	74
Skim milk	1 cup	255	19	200	29	1	0.3	0.2	tr	9
Dried:										
Buttermilk	1 cup	120	41	465	59	7	4.3	2.0	0.3	83
Nonfat, instant:										
Envelope, 3.2 oz	1	91	32	325	47	1	0.4	0.2	tr	17
cup	1 cup	68	24	245	35	tr	0.3	0.1	tr	12

Dairy Products continued

Milk beverages:

Foods	Approximate Measure Portion	Weight Grams	Calories Calories	Protein Grams	Carbohydrate Grams	Total Fat Grams	Fats Saturated Grams	Fats Mono-unsaturated Grams	Fats Poly-unsaturated Grams	Cholesterol Milligrams
Chocolate milk (comm):										
Regular . . . . .1 cup		250	210	8	26	8	5.3	2.5	0.3	31
Low fat (2%) . . . . . . .1 cup		250	180	8	26	5	3.1	1.5	0.2	17
Lowfat (1%) . . . . . . .1 cup		250	160	8	26	3	1.5	0.8	0.1	7
Cocoa & chocolate flavored										
Powder containing nonfat										
dry milk . . . . .1 oz		28	100	3	22	1	0.6	0.3	tr	1
Prepared (6 oz. water										
+ 1 oz. powder) . . . . .1 serv		206	100	3	22	1	0.6	0.3	tr	1
Powder without nonfat										
dry milk . . . . ¾ oz		21	75	1	19	1	0.3	0.2	tr	0
Prepared (8 oz. whole milk										
+ ¾ oz. powder) . . . . .1 serv		265	225	9	30	9	5.4	2.5	0.3	33
Eggnog (commercial) . . . . .1 cup		254	340	10	4	19	11.3	5.7	0.9	149
Malted milk:										
Chocolate:										
Powder . . . . ¾ oz		21	85	1	18	1	0.5	0.3	0.1	1
Prepared (8 oz. whole milk										
+ ¾ oz. powder) . . . . .1 serv		265	235	9	29	9	5.5	2.7	0.4	34

Natural:									
Powder . . . . ¾ oz	21	85	3	15	2	0.9	0.5	0.3	4
Prepared (8 oz. whole milk + ¾ oz. powder) . . . . 1 serv	265	235	11	27	10	6.0	2.9	0.6	37
Shakes, thick:									
Chocolate . . . . .10 oz	283	335	9	60	8	4.8	2.2	0.3	33
Vanilla . . . . .10 oz	283	315	11	50	9	5.3	2.5	0.3	30
Yogurt:									
With added milk solids:									
Made with lowfat milk:									
Fruit flavored . . . . .8 oz	227	230	10	43	2	1.6	0.7	0.1	10
Plain . . . . .8 oz	227	145	12	16	4	2.3	1.0	0.1	14
Made with nonfat milk . . . . . .8 oz	227	125	13	17	tr	0.3	0.1	tr	4
Without added milk solids:									
Made with whole milk . . . . . . .8 oz	227	140	8	11	7	4.8	2.0	0.2	29

Eggs

Eggs, large:									
Raw:									
Whole . . . . .1 egg	50	80	6	1	6	1.7	2.2	0.7	210
White of egg 1	33	15	3	tr	tr	0.0	0.0	0.0	0
Yolk 1	17	65	3	tr	6	1.7	2.2	0.7	210
Cooked:									
Fried, in butter . . . . .1 egg	46	95	6	1	7	2.7	2.7	0.8	214
Hard-cooked 1	50	80	6	1	6	1.7	2.2	0.7	210
Poached 1	50	80	6	1	6	1.7	2.2	0.7	209
Scrambled or omelet, milk added, in butter . . . . .1 egg	64	110	7	2	8	3.2	2.9	0.8	218

Foods	Approximate Measure Portion	Weight Grams	Calories Calories	Protein Grams	Carbohydrate Grams	Total Fat Grams	Fats			Cholesterol Milligrams
							Saturated Grams	Mono-unsaturated Grams	Poly-unsaturated Grams	
Fats and Oils										
Fats, cooking (vegetable shortenings)............	1 cup	205	1,810	0	0	205	51.3	91.2	53.5	0
	1 Tbs	13	115	0	0	13	3.3	5.8	3.4	0
Lard....................	1 cup	205	1,850	0	0	205	80.4	92.5	23.0	195
	1 Tbs	13	115	0	0	13	5.1	5.9	1.5	12
Margarine:										
Imitation, about 40% fat, soft......1 Tbs	14	50	tr	tr	5	1.1	2.2	1.9	0
Regular, about 80% fat:										
Hard:										
stick..................	½ cup	113	810	1	1	91	17.9	40.5	28.7	0
	1 Tbs.	14	100	tr	tr	11	2.2	5.0	3.6	0
1" sq. pat..........	1 pat	5	35	tr	tr	4	0.8	1.8	1.3	0
Soft..............	1 Tbs	14	100	tr	tr	11	1.9	4.0	4.8	0
Spread, about 60% fat:										
Hard:										
Stick...............	½ cup	113	610	1	0	69	15.9	29.4	20.5	0
	1 Tbs	14	75	tr	0	9	2.0	3.6	2.5	0
1" sq. pat.........	1 pat	5	25	tr	0	3	0.7	1.3	0.9	0
Soft..............	1 Tbs	14	75	tr	0	9	1.8	4.4	1.9	0
Oils, salad or cooking:										
Canola.............	1 Tbs	14	125	0	0	14	1.0	9.0	4.0	0
Coconut............	1 Tbs	14	117	0	0	14	12.0	1.0	0.2	0
Corn...............	1 Tbs	14	125	0	0	14	1.8	3.4	8.2	0

		Grams	Calories	Protein	Carbohydrate	Fat	Saturated	Monounsaturated	Polyunsaturated	Cholesterol
Olive	1 Tbs	14	125	0	0	14	1.9	10.3	1.2	0
Palm	1 Tbs	14	120	0	0	14	7.0	5.0	1.0	0
Peanut	1 Tbs	14	125	0	0	14	2.4	6.5	4.5	0
Safflower	1 Tbs	14	125	0	0	14	1.3	1.7	10.4	0
Soybean oil, partially hydrogenated	1 Tbs	14	125	0	0	14	2.1	6.0	5.3	0
Soybean-cottonseed oil blend, partially hydrogenated	1 Tbs	14	125	0	0	14	2.5	4.1	6.7	0
Sunflower	1 Tbs	14	125	0	0	14	1.4	2.7	9.2	0
Salad dressings:										
Commercial:										
Blue cheese	1 Tbs	15	75	1	1	8	1.5	1.8	4.2	3
French:										
Regular	1 Tbs	16	85	tr	1	9	1.4	4.0	3.5	0
Low calorie	1 Tbs	16	25	tr	2	2	0.2	0.3	1.0	0
Italian:										
Regular	1 Tbs	15	80	tr	1	9	1.3	3.7	3.2	0
Low calorie	1 Tbs	15	5	tr	2	tr	tr	tr	tr	0
Mayonnaise:										
Regular	1 Tbs	14	100	tr	tr	11	1.7	3.2	5.8	8
Imitation	1 Tbs	15	35	tr	2	3	0.5	0.7	1.6	4
Mayonnaise type	1 Tbs	15	60	tr	4	5	0.7	1.4	2.7	4
Tartar	1 Tbs	14	75	tr	1	8	1.2	2.6	3.9	4

Fats and Oils continued

Foods	Approximate Measure	Weight	Calories	Protein	Carbohydrate	Total Fat	Fats Saturated	Mono-unsaturated	Poly-unsaturated	Cholesterol
	Portion	Grams	Calories	Grams	Grams	Grams	Grams	Grams	Grams	Milligrams
Thousand island:										
Regular..........1 Tbs		16	60	tr	2	6	1.0	1.3	3.2	4
Low calorie..........1 Tbs		15	25	tr	2	2	0.2	0.4	0.9	2
Prepared from own recipe:										
Cooked type..........1 Tbs		16	25	1	2	2	0.5	0.6	0.3	9
Vinegar & oil..........1 Tbs		16	70	0	tr	8	1.5	2.4	3.9	0

Fish and Shellfish

Foods	Approximate Measure	Weight	Calories	Protein	Carbohydrate	Total Fat	Fats Saturated	Mono-unsaturated	Poly-unsaturated	Cholesterol
Clams:										
Raw, meat only..........3 oz		85	65	11	2	1	0.3	0.3	0.3	43
Canned, drained..........3 oz		85	85	13	2	2	0.5	0.5	0.4	54
Crabmeat, canned..........1 cup		135	135	23	1	3	0.5	0.8	1.4	135
Fish sticks..........1 stick		28	70	6	4	3	0.8	1.4	0.8	26
Flounder or Sole, baked with lemon juice:										
With butter..........3 oz		85	120	16	tr	6	3.2	1.5	0.5	68
With margarine..........3 oz		85	120	16	tr	6	1.2	2.3	1.9	59
Without added fat..........3 oz		85	80	17	tr	1	0.3	0.2	0.4	55
Haddock, breaded, fried..........3 oz		85	175	17	tr	9	2.4	3.9	2.4	75
Halibut, broiled, with butter & lemon juice..........3 oz		85	140	20	tr	6	3.3	1.6	0.7	62
Herring, pickled..........3 oz		85	190	17	0	13	4.3	4.6	3.1	85
Ocean perch, breaded, fried..........1 fillet		85	185	16	7	11	2.6	4.6	2.8	66

Food	Measure									
Oysters:										
Raw, meat only	1 cup	240	160	20	8	4	1.4	0.5	1.4	120
Breaded, fried	1 oyster	45	90	5	5	5	1.4	2.1	1.4	35
Salmon:										
Canned (pink), solids & liquid	3 oz	85	120	17	0	5	0.9	1.5	2.1	34
Baked (red)	3 oz	85	140	21	0	5	1.2	2.4	1.4	60
Smoked	3 oz	85	150	18	0	8	2.6	3.9	0.7	51
Sardines, Atlantic, canned										
in oil, drained	3 oz	85	175	20	0	9	2.1	3.7	2.9	85
Scallops, breaded	6	90	195	15	10	10	2.5	4.1	2.5	70
Shrimp:										
Canned, drained	3 oz	85	100	21	1	1	0.2	0.2	0.4	128
French fried, 7 med.	3 oz	85	200	16	11	10	2.5	4.1	2.6	168
Trout, broiled, with butter										
and lemon juice	3 oz	85	175	21	tr	9	4.1	2.9	1.6	71
Tuna, canned, drained:										
Oil packed, chunk light	3 oz	85	165	24	0	7	1.4	1.9	3.1	55
Water packed, solid white	3 oz	85	135	30	0	1	0.3	0.2	0.3	48
Tuna salad	1 cup	205	375	33	19	19	3.3	4.9	9.2	80

Fruit and Fruit Juices

Food	Measure									
Apples:										
Raw:										
Unpeeled, without core:										
2¾″ diam	1 apple	138	80	tr	21	tr	0.1	tr	0.1	0
3¼″ diam	1 apple	212	125	tr	32	1	0.1	tr	0.2	0
Peeled, sliced	1 cup	110	65	tr	16	tr	0.1	tr	0.1	0
Dried, sulfured	10 rings	64	155	1	42	tr	tr	tr	0.1	0
Apple juice	1 cup	248	115	tr	29	tr	tr	tr	0.1	0

Fruit and Fruit Juices continued

Foods	Approximate Measure Portion	Weight Grams	Calories Calories	Protein Grams	Carbohydrate Grams	Total Fat Grams	Fats Saturated Grams	Mono-unsaturated Grams	Poly-unsaturated Grams	Cholesterol Milligrams
Applesauce, canned:										
Sweetened ....1 cup	255	195	tr	51	tr	0.1	tr	0.1	0
Unsweetened..............1 cup	244	105	tr	28	tr	tr	tr	tr	0
Apricots:										
Raw 3	106	50	1	12	tr	tr	0.2	0.1	0
Canned (fruit & liquid):										
Heavy syrup pack ....1 cup	258	215	1	55	tr	tr	0.1	tr	0
3 halves	85	70	tr	18	tr	tr	tr	tr	0
Juice pack ....1 cup	248	120	2	31	tr	tr	tr	tr	0
3 halves	84	40	1	10	tr	tr	tr	tr	0
Dried:										
Uncooked ....1 cup	130	310	5	80	1	tr	0.3	0.1	0
Cooked, unsweetened, fruit & liquid ....1 cup	250	210	3	55	tr	tr	0.2	0.1	0
Apricot nectar ....1 cup	251	140	1	36	tr	tr	0.1	tr	0
Avocados, raw:										
California, 2/lb........ 1 avocado	173	305	4	12	30	4.5	19.4	3.5	0
Florida, 1/lb .... 1 avocado	304	340	5	27	27	5.3	14.8	4.5	0
Bananas, 2 ½/lb ...... 1 banana	114	105	1	27	1	0.2	tr	0.1	0
Sliced.................1 cup	150	140	2	35	1	0.3	0.1	0.1	0
Blackberries, raw ......1 cup	144	75	1	18	1	0.2	0.1	0.1	0
Blueberries:										
Raw ....1 cup	145	80	1	20	1	tr	0.1	0.3	0
Frozen, sweetened .....1 cup	230	185	1	50	tr	tr	tr	tr	0
Cantaloupe, 5" diam .... ½ melon	267	95	2	22	1	0.1	0.1	0.3	0

Food	Measure	g								
Cherries:										
Sour, red, pitted, canned, water pack	1 cup	244	90	2	22	tr	0.1	0.1	0.1	0
Sweet, raw	10	68	50	1	11	1	0.1	0.2	0.2	0
Cranberry juice cocktail, bottled, sweetened	1 cup	253	145	tr	38	tr	tr	tr	0.1	0
Cranberry sauce, sweetened, canned, strained	1 cup	277	420	1	108	tr	tr	0.1	0.2	0
Dates:										
Whole	10 dates	83	230	2	61	tr	0.1	0.1	tr	0
Chopped	1 cup	178	490	4	131	1	0.3	0.2	tr	0
Figs, dried	10 figs	187	475	6	122	2	0.4	0.5	1.0	0
Fruit cocktail, canned, fruit and liquid:										
Heavy syrup pack	1 cup	255	185	1	48	tr	tr	tr	0.1	0
Juice pack	1 cup	248	115	1	29	tr	tr	tr	tr	0
Grapefruit:										
Raw, 3¾″ diam	½	120	40	1	10	tr	tr	tr	tr	0
Canned, with syrup	1 cup	254	150	1	39	tr	tr	tr	0.1	0
Grapefruit juice:										
Fresh	1 cup	247	95	1	23	tr	tr	tr	0.1	0
Canned:										
Unsweetened	1 cup	247	95	1	22	tr	tr	tr	0.1	0
Sweetened	1 cup	250	115	1	28	tr	tr	tr	0.1	0
Frozen concentrate, unsweetened:										
Undiluted	6 oz can	207	300	4	72	1	0.1	0.1	0.2	0
Diluted with 3 parts water by volume	1 cup	247	100	1	24	tr	tr	tr	0.1	0
Grapes, raw:										
Thompson Seedless	10 grapes	50	35	tr	9	tr	0.1	tr	0.1	0

Fruit and Fruit Juices continued

Foods	Approximate Measure Portion	Weight Grams	Calories	Protein Grams	Carbohydrate Grams	Total Fat Grams	Fats Saturated Grams	Fats Mono-unsaturated Grams	Fats Poly-unsaturated Grams	Cholesterol Milligrams
Tokay & Emperor, seeded types ....10 grapes	57	40	tr	10	tr	0.1	tr	0.1	0
Grape juice:									
Canned or bottled ....1 cup	253	155	1	38	tr	0.1	tr	0.1	0
Frozen concentrate, sweetened:									
Undiluted.............6 oz can	216	385	1	96	1	0.2	tr	0.2	0
Diluted with 3 parts water by volume...........1 cup	250	125	tr	32	tr	0.1	tr	0.1	0
Honeydew, 6½″ diam.........1/10 melon	129	45	1	12	tr	tr	tr	0.1	0
Kiwifruit, raw, 5/lb.........1 kiwi	76	45	1	11	tr	tr	0.1	0.1	0
Lemons, 4/lb ....1 lemon	58	15	1	5	tr	tr	tr	0.1	0
Lemon juice:									
Fresh.................1 cup	244	60	1	21	tr	tr	tr	tr	0
Canned or bottled, unsweetened ...1 cup	244	50	1	16	1	0.1	tr	0.2	0
1 Tbs	15	5	tr	1	tr	tr	tr	tr	0
Frozen, single-strength, unsweetened ....6 oz can	244	55	1	16	1	0.1	tr	0.2	0
Lime juice:									
Fresh ....1 cup	246	65	1	22	tr	tr	tr	0.1	0
Canned, unsweetened...........1 cup	246	50	1	16	1	0.1	0.1	0.2	0
Mangos, 1½/lb.........1 mango	207	135	1	35	1	0.1	0.2	0.1	0
Nectarines, 3/lb ....1 nect.	136	65	1	16	1	0.1	0.2	0.3	0
Oranges:									
Whole, 2⅝″ diam..........1 orange	131	60	1	15	tr	tr	tr	tr	0
sections................1 cup	180	85	2	21	tr	tr	tr	tr	0

Food	Measure									
Orange juice:										
Fresh	1 cup	248	110	2	26	tr	0.1	0.1	0.1	0
Canned, unsweetened	1 cup	249	105	1	25	tr	tr	0.1	0.1	0
Frozen concentrate:										
Undiluted	6 oz can	213	340	5	81	tr	0.1	0.1	0.1	0
Diluted, 3 parts water by volume	1 cup	249	110	2	27	tr	tr	tr	tr	0
Orange & grapefruit juice canned	1 cup	247	105	1	25	tr	tr	tr	tr	0
Papayas, raw, cubed	1 cup	140	65	1	17	tr	0.1	tr	tr	0
Peaches:										
Raw, 2½″ diam	1 peach	87	35	1	10	tr	tr	tr	tr	0
Sliced	1 cup	170	75	1	19	tr	tr	0.1	0.1	0
Canned, fruit & liquid:										
Heavy syrup	1 cup	256	190	1	51	tr	tr	0.1	0.1	0
	½	81	60	tr	16	tr	tr	tr	tr	0
Juice pack	1 cup	248	110	2	29	tr	tr	tr	tr	0
	½	77	35	tr	9	tr	tr	tr	tr	0
Dried:										
Uncooked	1 cup	160	380	6	98	1	0.1	0.4	0.6	0
Cooked, unsweetened with liquid	1 cup	258	200	3	51	1	0.1	0.2	0.3	0
Frozen, sliced, sweetened	1 cup	250	235	2	60	tr	tr	0.1	0.2	0
Pears:										
Bartlett 2½″ diam	1 pear	166	100	1	25	1	tr	0.1	0.2	0
Bosc 2½″ diam	1 pear	141	85	1	21	1	tr	0.1	0.1	0
D'Anjou 3″ diam	1 pear	200	120	1	30	1	tr	0.2	0.2	0
Canned, fruit & liquid:										
Heavy syrup pack	1 cup	255	190	1	49	tr	tr	0.1	0.1	0
	½	79	60	tr	15	tr	tr	tr	tr	0

Fruit and Fruit Juices continued

Foods	Approximate Measure Portion	Weight Grams	Calories Calories	Protein Grams	Carbohydrate Grams	Total Fat Grams	Fats Saturated Grams	Mono-unsaturated Grams	Poly-unsaturated Grams	Cholesterol Milligrams
Juice pack...........................1 cup		248	125	1	32	tr	tr	tr	tr	0
½		77	40	tr	10	tr	tr	tr	tr	0
Pineapple:										
Raw, diced ....1 cup		155	75	1	19	1	tr	0.1	0.2	0
Canned, fruit & liquid:										
Heavy syrup pack:										
Crushed, chunks, tibits........1 cup		255	200	1	52	tr	tr	tr	0.1	0
Slices ....1 slice		58	45	tr	12	tr	tr	tr	tr	0
Juice pack:										
Crushed, chunks, tibits........1 cup		250	150	1	39	tr	tr	tr	0.1	0
Slices ....1 slice		58	35	tr	9	tr	tr	tr	tr	0
Pineapple juice, unsweetened, canned.........................1 cup		250	140	1	34	tr	tr	tr	tr	0
Plantains:										
Raw 1		179	220	2	57	1	0.3	0.1	0.1	0
Cooked, sliced..............1 cup		154	180	1	48	tr	0.1	tr	0.1	0
Plums:										
Raw:										
2⅛" diam............ 1 plum		66	35	1	9	tr	tr	0.3	0.1	0
1½" diam............ 1 plum		28	15	tr	4	tr	tr	0.1	tr	0
Canned, purple, fruit and liquid:										
Heavy syrup pack ....1 cup		258	230	1	60	tr	tr	0.2	0.1	0
3 plums		133	120	tr	31	tr	tr	0.1	tr	0
Juice pack...............1 cup		252	145	1	38	tr	tr	tr	tr	0
3 plums		95	55	tr	14	tr	tr	tr	tr	0

Food	Measure									
Prunes, dried:										
Uncooked	4 x-large or 5 large	49	115	1	31	tr	tr	0.2	0.1	0
Cooked, unsweetened, with liquid	1 cup	212	225	2	60	tr	tr	0.3	0.1	0
Prune juice, canned	1 cup	256	180	2	45	tr	tr	0.1	tr	0
Raisins, seedless:										
Not pressed down	1 cup	145	435	5	115	1	0.2	tr	0.2	0
Packet, ½ oz	1½ Tbs	14	40	tr	11	tr	tr	tr	tr	0
Raspberries:										
Raw	1 cup	123	60	1	14	1	tr	0.1	0.4	0
Frozen, sweetened	1 cup	250	255	2	65	tr	tr	tr	0.2	0
Rhubarb, cooked, sugar added	1 cup	240	280	1	75	tr	tr	tr	0.1	0
Strawberries:										
Raw, whole	1 cup	149	45	1	10	1	tr	0.1	0.3	0
Frozen, sweetened, sliced	1 cup	255	245	1	66	tr	tr	tr	0.2	0
Tangerines:										
Raw, 2⅜" diam	1 tangerine	84	35	1	9	tr	tr	tr	tr	0
Canned, light syrup, fruit & liquid	1 cup	252	155	1	41	tr	tr	tr	0.1	0
Tangerine juice, canned, sweetened	1 cup	249	125	1	30	tr	tr	tr	0.1	0
Watermelon, raw:										
4 x 8" wedge	1 piece	482	155	3	35	2	0.3	0.2	1.0	0
Diced	1 cup	160	50	1	11	1	0.1	0.1	0.3	0

Grain Products

Food	Measure									
Bagel, plain or water, enriched, 3½" diam	1 bagel	68	200	7	38	2	0.3	0.5	0.7	0

Grain Products continued

Foods	Approximate Measure Portion	Weight Grams	Calories Calories	Protein Grams	Carbohydrate Grams	Total Fat Grams	Fats Saturated Grams	Mono-unsaturated Grams	Poly-unsaturated Grams	Cholesterol Milligrams
Barley, pearled, light uncooked ....1 cup		200	700	16	158	2	0.3	0.2	0.9	0
Biscuits, baking powder 2″ diam (enriched flour, veg. short.):										
From home recipe ....1 biscuit		28	100	2	13	5	1.2	2.0	1.3	tr
From mix ....1 biscuit		28	95	2	14	3	0.8	1.4	0.9	tr
From refrig. dough ....1 biscuit		20	65	1	10	2	0.6	0.9	0.6	1
Breadcrumbs, enriched:										
Dry, grated ....1 cup		100	390	13	73	5	1.5	1.6	1.0	5
Soft ....1 cup		45	120	4	22	2	0.6	0.6	0.4	0
Breads:										
Boston Brown, canned, sliced ......1 slice		45	95	2	21	1	0.3	0.1	0.1	3
Cracked-wheat ....1 slice		25	65	2	12	1	0.2	0.2	0.3	1
French 5 x 2½ x 1″ ....1 slice		35	100	3	18	1	0.3	0.4	0.5	0
Vienna 4¾ x 4 x ½″ ....1 slice		25	70	2	13	1	0.2	0.3	0.3	0
Italian 4½ x 3¼ x ¾″ ....1 slice		30	85	3	17	tr	tr	tr	0.1	0
Mixed grain, enriched:										
Slices, 18/loaf ....1 slice		25	65	2	12	1	0.2	0.2	0.4	0
Toasted ....1 slice		23	65	2	12	1	0.2	0.2	0.4	0
Oatmeal:										
Slices 18/loaf..................1 slice		25	65	2	12	1	0.2	0.4	0.5	0
Toasted ....1 slice		23	65	2	12	1	0.2	0.4	0.5	0
Pita 6½″ diam.................1 pita		60	165	6	33	1	0.1	0.1	0.4	0
Pumpernickel:										
Slice 5 x 4 x ⅜″..............1 slice		32	80	3	16	1	0.2	0.3	0.5	0
Toasted ....1 slice		29	80	3	16	1	0.2	0.3	0.5	0

Food	Measure								
Raisin, enriched:									
Slice 18/loaf	1 slice	25	65	2	13	1	0.2	0.3	0.4	0
Toasted	1 slice	21	65	2	13	1	0.2	0.3	0.4	0
Rye, light:									
Slice 4¾ x 3¾ x 7/16	1 slice	25	65	2	12	1	0.2	0.3	0.3	0
Wheat bread, enriched:									
18 slices/loaf	1 slice	25	65	2	12	1	0.2	0.4	0.3	0
White bread, enriched:									
18 slices/loaf	1 slice	25	65	2	12	1	0.3	0.4	0.2	0
Cubes	1 cup	30	80	2	15	1	0.4	0.4	0.3	0
Whole Wheat:									
16 slices/loaf	1 slice	28	70	3	13	1	0.4	0.4	0.3	0
Bread stuffing, from mix:									
Dry type	1 cup	140	500	9	50	31	6.1	13.3	9.6	0
Moist type	1 cup	203	420	9	40	26	5.3	11.3	8.0	67
Breakfast cereals:									
Hot type:									
Corn (hominy) grits:									
Regular & enriched	1 cup	242	145	3	31	tr	tr	0.1	0.2	0
Instant, plain	1 pkt	137	80	2	18	tr	tr	tr	0.1	0
Cream of Wheat:									
Regular, quick, instant	1 cup	244	140	4	29	tr	0.1	tr	0.2	0
Mix'n Eat, plain	1 pkt.	142	100	3	21	tr	tr	tr	0.1	0
Malt-O-Meal	1 cup	240	120	4	26	tr	tr	tr	0.1	0
Oatmeal or rolled oats:									
Regular, quick, instant, nonfortified	1 cup	234	145	6	25	2	0.4	0.8	1.0	0
Instant, fortified:									
Plain	1 pkt	177	105	4	18	2	0.3	0.6	0.7	0
Flavored	1 pkt	164	160	5	31	2	0.3	0.7	0.8	0

Grain Products continued

Foods	Approximate Measure Portion	Weight Grams	Calories Calories	Protein Grams	Carbohydrate Grams	Total Fat Grams	Fats Saturated Grams	Mono-unsaturated Grams	Poly-unsaturated Grams	Cholesterol Milligrams
Ready to eat:										
All-Bran........................	⅓ cup	28	70	4	21	1	0.1	0.1	0.3	0
Cap'n Crunch	¾ cup	28	120	1	23	3	1.7	0.3	0.4	0
Cheerios	1¼ cup	28	110	4	20	2	0.3	0.6	0.7	0
Corn Flakes:										
Kellogg's	1¼ cup	28	110	2	24	tr	tr	tr	tr	0
Toasties	1¼ cup	28	110	2	24	tr	tr	tr	tr	0
40% Bran Flakes:										
Kellogg's	¾ cup	28	90	4	22	1	0.1	0.1	0.3	0
Post	⅔ cup	28	90	3	22	tr	0.1	0.1	0.2	0
Froot Loops	1 cup	28	110	2	25	1	0.2	0.1	0.1	0
Golden Grahams...............	¾ cup	28	110	2	24	1	0.7	0.1	0.2	tr
Grape-Nuts	¼ cup	28	100	3	23	tr	tr	tr	0.1	0
Honey Nut Cheerios	¾ cup	28	105	3	23	1	0.1	0.3	0.3	0
Lucky Charms..................	1 cup	28	110	3	23	1	0.2	0.4	0.4	0
Nature Valley Granola..........	⅓ cup	28	125	3	19	5	3.3	0.7	0.7	0
100% Natural Cereal	¼ cup	28	135	3	18	6	4.1	1.2	0.5	tr
Product 19	¾ cup	28	110	3	24	tr	tr	tr	0.1	0
Raisin Bran:										
Kellogg's	¾ cup	28	90	3	21	1	0.1	0.1	0.3	0
Post	½ cup	28	85	3	21	1	0.1	0.1	0.3	0
Rice Krispies	1 cup	28	110	2	25	tr	tr	tr	0.1	0
Shredded Wheat................	⅔ cup	28	100	3	23	1	0.1	0.1	0.3	0
Special K.......................	1⅓ cup	28	110	6	21	tr	tr	tr	tr	tr

Super Sugar Crisp . . . . ⅞ cup	28	105	2	26	tr	tr	tr	tr	0.1	0
Sugar Frosted Flakes:										
Kellogg's . . . . ¾ cup	28	110	1	26	tr	tr	tr	tr	tr	0
Sugar Smacks . . . . ¾ cup	28	105	2	25	1	0.1	0.1	0.1	0.2	0
Total . . . . 1 cup	28	100	3	22	1	0.1	0.1	0.1	0.3	0
Trix . . . . 1 cup	28	110	2	25	tr	0.2	0.1	tr	0.1	0
Wheaties . . . . 1 cup	28	100	3	23	tr	0.1	0.1	0.2	0.2	0
Buckwheat flour, light, sifted . . . . . . 1 cup	98	340	6	78	1	0.2	0.4	0.4	0.4	0
Bulgur, uncooked . . . . 1 cup	170	600	19	129	3	1.2	0.3	0.3	1.2	0
Cakes:										
Cakes prepared from mixes:										
Angelfood, 9¾″ diam.										
¹⁄₁₂ of cake . . . . 1 slice	53	125	3	29	tr	tr	tr	tr	0.1	0
Coffeecake, crumb 7¾ x 5⅝ × 1¼:										
⅙ of cake. . . . . 1 slice	72	230	5	38	7	2.0	2.8	1.6	1.6	47
Devil's food 9″ diam., chocolate										
icing; ¹⁄₁₆ of cake . . . . . . 1 slice	69	235	3	40	8	3.5	3.2	1.2	1.2	37
Cupcake, 2½″ diam. . . . . 1 cupcake	35	120	2	20	4	1.8	1.6	0.6	0.6	19
Gingerbread, 8″ sq.:										
⅑ of cake. . . . . 1 piece	63	175	2	32	4	1.1	1.8	1.2	1.2	1
Yellow 9″ diam., chocolate										
icing; ¹⁄₁₆ of cake . . . . 1 piece	69	235	3	40	8	3.0	3.0	1.4	1.4	36
Cakes prepared from home recipe:										
Carrot, 10″ diam with										
cream cheese icing:										
¹⁄₁₆ cake . . . . 1 piece	96	385	4	48	21	4.1	8.4	6.7	6.7	74
Fruitcake, dark, tube cake:										
¹⁄₃₂ of cake . . . . 1 piece	43	165	2	25	7	1.5	3.6	1.6	1.6	20

Grain Products continued

Foods	Approximate Measure	Weight	Calories	Protein	Carbohydrate	Total Fat	Fats Saturated	Mono-unsaturated	Poly-unsaturated	Cholesterol
	Portion	Grams	Calories	Grams	Grams	Grams	Grams	Grams	Grams	Milligrams
Plain sheet cake, 9" sq.:										
Without icing:										
⅑ of cake............1 piece		86	315	4	48	12	3.3	5.0	2.8	61
With uncooked white icing:										
⅑ of cake:............1 piece		121	445	4	77	14	4.6	5.6	2.9	70
Pound, 8½ x 3½ x 3¼":										
1/17 of loaf............1 slice		30	120	2	15	5	1.2	2.4	1.6	32
Cakes, commercial:										
Pound, 8½ x 3½ x 3":										
1/17 of loaf............1 slice		29	110	2	15	5	3.0	1.7	0.2	64
Snack cakes:										
Devil's food with cream filling, 2/pack............1 cake		28	105	1	17	4	1.7	1.5	0.6	15
Sponge with cream filling 2/pack............1 cake		42	155	1	27	5	2.3	2.1	0.5	7
White, 8 or 9" diam. with white icing: 1/16 of cake......1 piece		71	260	3	42	9	2.1	3.8	2.6	3
Yellow, 8 or 9" diam. with chocolate icing: 1/16 of cake............1 piece		69	245	2	39	11	5.7	3.7	0.6	38
Cheesecake, 9" diam.: 1/12 of cake............1 piece		92	280	5	26	18	9.9	5.4	1.2	170

Cookies:

Food	Measure	Weight (g)		Calories						
Brownies with nuts:										
Commercial with icing, 1½ x 1¾ x ⅞"	1 brownie	25	1	100	16	4	1.6	2.0	0.6	14
Home recipe, 1¾ x 1¾ x ⅞"	1 brownie	20	1	95	11	6	1.4	2.8	1.2	18
Chocolate chip:										
Commercial, 2¼" diam. ⅜" thick	4 cookies	42	2	180	28	9	2.9	3.1	2.6	5
Home recipe, 2⅓" diam	4 cookies	40	2	185	26	11	3.9	4.3	2.0	18
From refrig. dough, 2¼" diam	4 cookies	48	2	225	32	11	4.0	4.4	2.0	22
Fig bars, square, 1⅝ x 1⅝ x ⅜"	4 cookies	56	2	210	42	4	1.0	1.5	1.0	27
Oatmeal with raisins, 2⅝" diam	4 cookies	52	3	245	36	10	2.5	4.5	2.8	2
Peanut butter cookie, home recipe, 2⅝" diam	4 cookies	48	4	245	28	14	4.0	5.8	2.8	22
Sandwich type, choc. or vanilla, 1¾" diam., ⅜" thick	4 cookies	40	2	195	29	8	2.0	3.6	2.2	0
Shortbread:										
Commercial	4 sm. cookies	32	2	155	20	8	2.9	3.0	1.1	27
Home recipe	2 lg. cookies	28	2	145	17	8	1.3	2.7	3.4	0
Sugar cookie, from refrig. dough 2½" diam., ¼" thick	4 cookies	48	2	235	31	12	2.3	5.0	3.6	29
Vanilla wafers, 1¾" diam., ¼" thick	10 cookies	40	2	185	29	7	1.8	3.0	1.8	25
Corn chips	1 oz pack.	28	2	155	16	9	1.4	2.4	3.7	0
Cornmeal:										
Whole-ground, unbolted, dry form	1 cup	122	11	435	90	5	0.5	1.1	2.5	0

Grain Products continued

Foods	Approximate Measure / Portion	Weight Grams	Calories Calories	Protein Grams	Carbohydrate Grams	Total Fat Grams	Fats Saturated Grams	Mono-unsaturated Grams	Poly-unsaturated Grams	Cholesterol Milligrams
Bolted, dry form............	1 cup	122	440	11	91	4	0.5	0.9	2.2	0
Degermed, enriched:										
Dry form............	1 cup	138	500	11	108	2	0.2	0.4	0.9	0
Cooked............	1 cup	240	120	3	26	tr	tr	0.1	0.2	0
Crackers:										
Cheese:										
Plain, 1" sq............	10 crackers	10	50	1	6	3	0.9	1.2	0.3	6
Sandwich type, peanut butter............	1 sandwich	8	40	1	5	2	0.4	0.8	0.3	1
Graham, plain, 2½" sq.........	2 crackers	14	60	1	11	1	0.4	0.6	0.4	0
Melba toast, plain.........	1 piece	5	20	1	4	tr	0.1	0.1	0.1	0
Rye wafers, whole-grain, 1⅞ x 3½"	2 wafers	14	55	1	10	1	0.3	0.4	0.3	0
Saltines............	4 crackers	12	50	1	9	1	0.5	0.4	0.2	4
Snack type, standard cracker.....	1 round	3	15	tr	2	1	0.2	0.4	0.1	0
Wheat, thin............	4 crackers	8	35	1	5	1	0.5	0.5	0.4	0
Whole-wheat wafers............	2 crackers	8	35	1	5	2	0.5	0.6	0.4	0
Croissants 4½ x 4 x 1¾"............	1 croissant	57	235	5	27	12	3.5	6.7	1.4	13
Danish pastry:										
Plain without fruit or nuts:										
Round piece 4¼" diam., 1" high............	1 pastry	57	220	4	26	12	3.6	4.8	2.6	49
Ounce............	1 oz	28	110	2	13	6	1.8	2.4	1.3	24
Fruit, round piece............	1 pastry	65	235	4	28	13	3.9	5.2	2.9	56

Food	Amount								
Doughnuts:									
Cake type, plain, 3¼″ diam., 1″ high	1 doughnut	50	210	3	24	12	2.8	5.0	3.0	20
Yeast type, glazed, 3¾″ diam., 1″ high	1 doughnut	60	235	4	26	13	5.2	5.5	0.9	21
English muffin, plain	1 muffin	57	140	5	27	1	0.3	0.2	0.3	0
French toast, home recipe	1 slice	65	155	6	17	7	1.6	2.0	1.6	112
Macaroni, enriched, cooked (shells, elbows)										
Firm stage	1 cup	130	190	7	39	1	0.1	0.1	0.3	0
Tender stage:										
Cold	1 cup	105	115	4	24	tr	0.1	0.1	0.2	0
Hot	1 cup	140	155	5	32	1	0.1	0.1	0.2	0
Muffins made with enriched flour, 2½″ diam.										
Home recipe										
Blueberry	1 muffin	45	135	3	20	5	1.5	2.1	1.2	19
Bran	1 muffin	45	125	3	19	6	1.4	1.6	2.3	24
Corn (enriched degermed cornmeal & flour)	1 muffin	45	145	3	21	5	1.5	2.2	1.4	23
From mix (egg & water added):										
Blueberry	1 muffin	45	140	3	22	5	1.4	2.0	1.2	45
Bran	1 muffin	45	140	3	24	4	1.3	1.6	1.0	28
Corn	1 muffin	45	145	3	22	6	1.7	2.3	1.4	42
Noodles (egg) enriched, cooked	1 cup	160	200	7	37	2	0.5	0.6	0.6	50
Noodles, chow mein, canned	1 cup	45	220	6	26	11	2.1	7.3	0.4	5
Pancakes, 4″ diam.:										
Buckwheat, from mix, egg & milk added	1 pancake	27	55	2	6	2	0.9	0.9	0.5	20

Grain Products continued

Foods	Approximate Measure	Weight	Calories	Protein	Carbohydrate	Total Fat	Fats			Cholesterol
							Saturated	Mono-unsaturated	Poly-unsaturated	
	Portion	Grams	Calories	Grams	Grams	Grams	Grams	Grams	Grams	Milligrams
Plain:										
Home recipe .... 1 pancake		27	60	2	9	2	0.5	0.8	0.5	16
Mix, egg, milk & oil added........... 1 pancake		27	60	2	8	2	0.5	0.9	0.5	16
Piecrust, made with enriched flour, & veg. short., baked:										
Home recipe, 9″ diam........ 1 pie shell		180	900	11	79	60	14.8	25.9	15.7	0
From mix, 9″ diam .... piecrust for 2 crust pie		320	1,485	20	141	93	22.7	41.0	25.0	0
Pies, crust made with enriched flour & veg. short., 9″ diam.:										
Apple, ⅙ pie .... 1 piece		158	405	3	60	18	4.6	7.4	4.4	0
Blueberry, ⅙ pie .... 1 piece		158	380	4	55	17	4.3	7.4	4.6	0
Cherry, ⅙ pie............ 1 piece		158	410	4	61	18	4.7	7.7	4.6	0
Creme, ⅙ pie .... 1 piece		152	455	3	59	23	15.0	4.0	1.1	8
Custard, ⅙ pie .... 1 piece		152	330	9	36	17	5.6	6.7	3.2	169
Lemon meringue, ⅙ pie		140	355	5	53	14	4.3	5.7	2.9	143
Peach, ⅙ pie........... 1 piece		158	405	4	60	17	4.1	7.3	4.4	0
Pecan, ⅙ pie .... 1 piece		138	575	7	71	32	4.7	17.0	7.9	95
Pumpkin, ⅙ pie .... 1 piece		152	320	6	37	17	6.4	6.7	3.0	109
Pies, fried:										
Apple.................1 pie		85	255	2	31	14	5.8	6.6	0.6	14
Cherry................1 pie		85	250	2	32	14	5.8	6.7	0.6	13
Popcorn, popped:										
Air-popped, unsalted ....1 cup		8	30	1	6	tr	tr	0.1	0.2	0

Food	Measure								
Popped in veg. oil, salted	1 cup	11	55	1	6	3	0.5	1.4	1.2	0
Sugar syrup coated	1 cup	35	135	2	30	1	0.1	0.3	0.6	0
Pretzels:										
Stick, 2¼" long	10 sticks	3	10	tr	2	tr	tr	tr	tr	0
Twisted, dutch, 2¾ x 2⅝"	1 pretzel	16	65	2	13	1	0.1	0.2	0.2	0
Twisted, thin, 3¼ x 2¼ x ¼"	10 pretzels	60	240	6	48	2	0.4	0.8	0.6	0
Rice:										
Brown, cooked, hot	1 cup	195	230	5	50	1	0.3	0.3	0.4	0
White:										
Commercial varieties, all types:										
Raw	1 cup	185	670	12	149	1	0.2	0.2	0.3	0
Cooked, served hot	1 cup	205	225	4	50	tr	0.1	0.1	0.1	0
Instant, ready-to-serve, hot	1 cup	165	180	4	40	0	0.1	0.1	0.1	0
Parboiled:										
Raw	1 cup	185	685	14	150	1	0.1	0.1	0.2	0
Cooked, served hot	1 cup	175	185	4	41	tr	tr	tr	0.1	0
Rolls, enriched:										
Commercial:										
Dinner, 2½" diam., 2" high	1 roll	28	85	2	14	2	0.5	0.8	0.6	tr
Frankfurter & hamburger (8/pk)	1 roll	40	115	3	20	2	0.5	0.8	0.6	tr
Hard, 3¾" diam., 2" high	1 roll	50	155	5	30	2	0.4	0.5	0.6	tr
Hoagie, 11½ x 3 x 2½"	1 roll	135	400	11	72	8	1.8	3.0	2.2	tr
From home recipe:										
Dinner 2½ diam., 2" high	1 roll	35	120	3	20	3	0.8	1.2	0.9	12
Spaghetti, enriched, cooked:										
Firm stage, "al dente," served hot	1 cup	130	190	7	39	1	0.1	0.1	0.3	0
Tender stage, served hot	1 cup	140	155	5	32	1	0.1	0.1	0.2	0
Toaster pastries	1 pastry	54	210	2	38	6	1.7	3.6	0.4	0

Foods	Approximate Measure	Weight	Calories	Protein	Carbohydrate	Total Fat	Fats Saturated	Mono-unsaturated	Poly-unsaturated	Cholesterol
	Portion	Grams	Calories	Grams	Grams	Grams	Grams	Grams	Grams	Milligrams
Grain Products continued										
Tortilla, corn . . . . 1 tortilla		30	65	2	13	1	0.1	0.3	0.6	0
Waffles, made with enriched flour, 7" diam.:										
Home recipe . . . . 1 waffle		75	245	7	26	13	4.0	4.9	2.6	102
From mix, egg & milk added. . . . . 1 waffle		75	205	7	27	8	2.7	2.9	1.5	59
Wheat flours:										
All-purpose, enriched:										
Sifted, spooned . . . . 1 cup		115	420	12	88	1	0.2	0.1	0.5	0
Unsifted, spooned . . . . 1 cup		125	455	13	95	1	0.2	0.1	0.5	0
Cake or pastry flour. . . . . 1 cup		96	350	7	76	1	0.1	0.1	0.3	0
Self-rising, enriched, unsifted, spooned. . . . . 1 cup		125	440	12	93	1	0.2	0.1	0.5	0
Whole wheat, from hard wheats, stirred . . . . 1 cup		120	400	16	85	2	0.3	0.3	1.1	0
Legumes, Nuts and Seeds										
Almonds, shelled:										
Slivered, packed. . . . . 1 cup		135	795	27	28	70	6.7	45.8	14.8	0
Whole. . . . . 1 oz		28	167	6	6	15	1.4	9.6	3.1	0
Beans, dry:										
Cooked, drained:										
Black . . . . 1 cup		171	225	15	41	1	0.1	0.1	0.5	0
Great Northern . . . . 1 cup		180	210	14	38	1	0.1	0.1	0.6	0
Lima. . . . . 1 cup		190	260	16	49	1	0.2	0.1	0.5	0

Food	Amount								
Pea (navy)	1 cup	190	225	15	40	1	0.1	0.1	0.7	0
Pinto	1 cup	180	265	15	49	1	0.1	0.1	0.5	0
Canned, solids & liquid:									
White with:									
Frankfurters	1 cup	255	365	19	32	18	7.4	8.8	0.7	30
Pork & tomato sauce	1 cup	255	310	16	48	7	2.4	2.7	0.7	10
Pork & sweet sauce	1 cup	255	385	16	54	12	4.3	4.9	1.2	10
Red kidney	1 cup	255	230	15	42	1	0.1	0.1	0.6	0
Blackeyed peas, dry, cooked (with residual cooking liquid)	1 cup	250	190	13	35	1	0.2	tr	0.3	0
Brazil nuts, shelled	1 oz	28	185	4	4	19	4.6	6.5	6.8	0
Carob flour	1 cup	140	255	tr	126	tr	tr	0.1	0.1	0
Cashews nuts, salted:									
Dry roasted	1 cup	137	785	21	45	63	12.5	37.4	10.7	0
	1 oz	28	165	4	9	13	2.6	7.7	2.2	0
Roasted in oil	1 cup	130	750	21	37	63	12.4	36.9	10.6	0
	1 oz	28	165	5	8	14	2.7	8.1	2.3	0
Chestnuts, European, roasted, shelled	1 cup	143	350	5	76	3	0.6	1.1	1.2	0
Chickpeas, cooked, drained	1 cup	163	270	15	45	4	0.4	0.9	1.9	0
Coconut:									
Raw:									
Piece, 2 x 2 x ½"	1 piece	45	160	1	7	15	13.4	0.6	0.2	0
Shredded or grated	1 cup	80	285	3	12	27	23.8	1.1	0.3	0
Dried, sweetened, shredded	1 cup	93	470	3	44	33	29.3	1.4	0.4	0
Filberts (hazelnuts), chopped	1 cup	115	725	15	18	72	5.3	56.5	6.9	0
	1 oz	28	180	4	4	18	1.3	13.9	1.7	0
Lentils, dry cooked	1 cup	200	215	16	38	1	0.1	0.2	0.5	0
Macadamia nuts, roasted in oil, salted	1 cup	134	960	10	17	103	15.4	80.9	1.8	0
	1 oz	28	205	2	4	22	3.2	17.1	0.4	0

Legumes, Nuts and Seeds continued

| Foods | Approximate Measure | Weight | Calories | Protein | Carbohydrate | Total Fat | Fats | | | Cholesterol |
	Portion	Grams	Calories	Grams	Grams	Grams	Saturated Grams	Mono-unsaturated Grams	Poly-unsaturated Grams	Milligrams
Mixed nuts, with peanuts, salted:										
Dry roasted	1 oz	28	170	5	7	15	2.0	8.9	3.1	0
Roasted in oil	1 oz	28	175	5	6	16	2.5	9.0	3.8	0
Peanuts, roasted in oil, salted	1 cup	145	840	39	27	71	9.9	35.5	22.6	0
	1 oz	28	165	8	5	14	1.9	6.9	4.4	0
Peanut butter	1 Tbs	16	95	5	3	8	1.4	4.0	2.5	0
Peas, split, dry, cooked	1 cup	200	230	16	42	1	0.1	0.1	0.3	0
Pecans, halves	1 cup	108	720	8	20	73	5.9	45.5	18.1	0
	1 oz	28	190	2	5	19	1.5	12.0	4.7	0
Pine nuts (pinyons), shelled	1 oz	28	160	3	5	17	2.7	6.5	7.3	0
Pistachio nuts, dried, shelled	1 oz	28	165	6	7	14	1.7	9.3	2.1	0
Pumpkin & squash kernels, dry, hulled	1 oz	28	155	7	5	13	2.5	4.0	5.9	0
Refried beans, canned	1 cup	290	295	18	51	3	0.4	0.6	1.4	0
Sesame seeds, dry, hulled	1 Tbs	8	45	2	1	4	0.6	1.7	1.9	0
Soybeans, dry, cooked, drained	1 cup	180	235	20	19	10	1.3	1.9	5.3	0
Soybean products:										
Miso	1 cup	276	470	29	65	13	1.8	2.6	7.3	0
Tofu, piece 2½ x 2¾ x 1"	1 piece	120	85	9	3	5	0.7	1.0	2.9	0
Sunflower seeds, dry, hulled	1 oz	28	160	6	5	14	1.5	2.7	9.3	0
Tahini	1 Tbs	15	90	3	3	8	1.1	3.0	3.5	0
Walnuts:										
Black, chopped	1 cup	125	760	30	15	71	4.5	15.9	46.9	0
	1 oz	28	170	7	3	16	1.0	3.6	10.6	0

Food	Measure	(g)	Cal.							
English or Persian, chips	1 cup	120	770	17	22	74	6.7	17.0	47.0	0
	1 oz	28	180	4	5	18	1.6	4.0	11.1	0

Meats and Meat Products

Beef, cooked:
Cuts braised, simmered, or pot roasted:
Relatively fat such as chuck blade:

Food	Measure	(g)	Cal.							
Lean & fat, piece	3 oz	85	325	22	0	26	10.8	11.7	0.9	87
Lean only	2.2 oz	62	170	19	0	9	3.9	4.2	0.3	66

Relatively lean, such as bottom round:

Food	Measure	(g)	Cal.							
Lean & fat	3 oz	85	220	25	0	13	4.8	5.7	0.5	81
Lean only	2.8 oz	78	175	25	0	8	2.7	3.4	0.3	75

Ground beef, broiled patty:

Food	Measure	(g)	Cal.							
Lean	3 oz	85	230	21	0	16	6.2	6.9	0.6	74
Regular	3 oz	85	245	20	0	18	6.9	7.7	0.7	76
Heart, lean, braised	3 oz	85	150	24	0	5	1.2	0.8	1.6	164
Liver, fried	3 oz	85	185	23	7	7	2.5	3.6	1.3	410

Roast, oven cooked, no liquid added:
Relatively fat, such as rib:

Food	Measure	(g)	Cal.							
Lean & fat	3 oz	85	315	19	0	26	10.8	11.4	0.9	72
Lean only	2.2 oz	61	150	17	0	9	3.6	3.7	0.3	49

Relatively lean, such as eye of round:

Food	Measure	(g)	Cal.							
Lean & fat	3 oz	85	205	23	0	12	4.9	5.4	0.5	62
Lean only	2.6 oz	75	135	22	0	5	1.9	2.1	0.2	52

Steak:
Sirloin broiled:

Food	Measure	(g)	Cal.							
Lean & fat	3 oz	85	240	23	0	15	6.4	6.9	0.6	77
Lean only	2.5 oz	72	150	22	0	6	2.6	2.8	0.3	64

Meats and Meat Products continued

Foods	Approximate Measure — Portion	Weight Grams	Calories	Protein Grams	Carbohydrate Grams	Total Fat Grams	Fats — Saturated Grams	Fats — Mono-unsaturated Grams	Fats — Poly-unsaturated Grams	Cholesterol Milligrams
Beef, canned, corned	3 oz	85	185	22	0	10	4.2	4.9	0.4	80
Beef, dried, chipped	2.5 oz	72	145	24	0	4	1.8	2.0	0.2	46
Lamb, cooked:										
Chops:										
Arm, braised:										
Lean & fat	2.2 oz	63	220	20	0	15	6.9	6.0	0.9	77
Lean only	1.7 oz	48	135	17	0	7	2.9	2.6	0.4	59
Loin, broiled:										
Lean & fat	2.8 oz	80	235	22	0	16	7.3	6.4	1.0	78
Lean only	2.3 oz	64	140	19	0	6	2.6	2.4	0.4	60
Leg, roasted:										
Lean & fat	3 oz	85	205	22	0	13	5.6	4.9	0.8	78
Lean only	2.6 oz	73	140	20	0	6	2.4	2.2	0.4	65
Rib roasted:										
Lean & fat	3 oz	85	315	18	0	26	12.1	10.1	1.5	77
Lean only	2 oz	57	130	15	0	7	3.2	3.0	0.5	50
Pork, cured, cooked:										
Bacon:										
Regular	3 med slices	19	110	6	tr	9	3.3	4.5	1.1	16
Canadian-style	2 slices	46	85	11	1	4	1.3	1.9	0.4	27
Ham, light cure, roasted:										
Lean & fat	3 oz	85	205	18	0	14	5.1	6.7	1.5	53
Lean only	2.4 oz	68	105	17	0	4	1.3	1.7	0.4	37
Ham, canned, roasted	3 oz	85	140	18	tr	7	2.4	3.5	0.8	35

Food									
Luncheon meat:									
Canned, 3 x 2 x ½.............. 2 slices	42	140	5	1	13	4.5	6.0	1.5	26
Chopped ham,									
8 slices/6 oz. pack.......... 2 slices	42	95	7	0	7	2.4	3.4	0.9	21
Cooked ham, 8 slices/6 oz pack:									
Regular.................... 2 slices	57	105	10	2	6	1.9	2.8	0.7	32
Extra lean................. 2 slices	57	75	11	1	3	0.9	1.3	0.3	27
Pork, fresh, cooked:									
Chop, loin:									
Broiled:									
Lean & fat .... 3.1 oz	87	275	24	0	19	7.0	8.8	2.2	84
Lean only .... 2.5 oz	72	165	23	0	8	2.6	3.4	0.9	71
Pan fried:									
Lean & fat .... 3.1 oz	89	335	21	0	27	9.8	12.5	3.1	92
Lean only .... 2.4 oz	67	180	19	0	11	3.7	4.8	1.3	72
Ham (leg) roasted:									
Lean & fat .... 3 oz	85	250	21	0	18	6.4	8.1	2.0	79
Lean only .... 2.5 oz	72	160	20	0	8	2.7	3.6	1.0	68
Rib, roasted:									
Lean & fat .... 3 oz	85	270	21	0	20	7.2	9.2	2.3	69
Lean only .... 2.5 oz	71	175	20	0	10	3.4	4.4	1.2	56
Shoulder cut, braised:									
Lean & fat .... 3 oz	85	295	23	0	22	7.9	10.0	2.4	93
Lean only .... 2.4 oz	67	165	22	0	8	2.8	3.7	1.0	76
Sausages:									
Bologna, 8 slices/8 oz. pack .... 2 slices	57	180	7	2	16	6.1	7.6	1.4	31
Braunschweiger, 6 slices/									
6 oz. pack................. 2 slices	57	205	8	2	18	6.2	8.5	2.1	89
Brown & serve, 10–11/8 oz. pack ... 1 link	13	50	2	tr	5	1.7	2.2	0.5	9
Frankfurter, 10/lb .... 1 frank	45	145	5	1	13	4.8	6.2	1.2	23

Meat and Meat Products continued

Foods	Approximate Measure Portion	Weight Grams	Calories Calories	Protein Grams	Carbohydrate Grams	Total Fat Grams	Saturated Grams	Mono-unsaturated Grams	Poly-unsaturated Grams	Cholesterol Milligrams
Pork link, 16/lb . . . . 1 link		13	50	3	tr	4	1.4	1.8	0.5	11
Salami:										
Cooked type, 8 slices/										
8 oz. pack . . . . 2 slices		57	145	8	1	11	4.6	5.2	1.2	37
Dry type, slice, 12/4 oz pack . . . . . 2 slices		20	85	5	1	7	2.4	3.4	0.6	16
Sandwich spread (pork, beef) . . . . . 1 Tbs		15	35	1	2	3	0.9	1.1	0.4	6
Vienna sausage, 7/4 oz . . . . 1 sausage		16	45	2	tr	4	1.5	2.0	0.3	8
Veal, medium fat, cooked:										
Cutlet, broiled . . . . 3 oz		85	185	23	0	9	4.1	4.1	0.6	109
Rib, roasted . . . . 3 oz		85	230	23	0	14	6.0	6.0	1.0	109

Mixed Dishes and Fast Food

Foods	Approximate Measure Portion	Weight Grams	Calories Calories	Protein Grams	Carbohydrate Grams	Total Fat Grams	Saturated Grams	Mono-unsaturated Grams	Poly-unsaturated Grams	Cholesterol Milligrams
Mixed dishes:										
Beef and vegetable stew,										
from home recipe . . . . 1 cup		245	220	16	15	11	4.4	4.5	0.5	71
Beef potpie, home recipe,										
⅓ of 9″ diam. pie . . . . 1 piece		210	515	21	39	30	7.9	12.9	7.4	42
Chicken a la king, home recipe . . . . 1 cup		245	470	27	12	34	12.9	13.4	6.2	221
Chicken & Noodles, cooked										
from home recipe . . . . 1 cup		240	365	22	26	18	5.1	7.1	3.9	103
Chicken chow mein:										
Canned . . . . 1 cup		250	95	7	18	tr	0.1	0.1	0.8	8
Home recipe . . . . 1 cup		250	255	31	10	10	4.1	4.9	3.5	75
Chicken potpie, home recipe										
⅓ of 9″ pie . . . . 1 piece		232	545	23	42	31	10.3	15.5	6.6	56

Food	Measure								
Chili con carne with beans, canned	1 cup	255	340	19	31	16	5.8	7.2	1.0	28
Chop suey with beef & pork, home recipe	1 cup	250	300	26	13	17	4.3	7.4	4.2	68
Macaroni & cheese:										
Canned . . . . 1 cup	1 cup	240	230	9	26	10	4.7	2.9	1.3	24
Home recipe . . . . 1 cup	1 cup	200	430	17	40	22	9.8	7.4	3.6	44
Quiche Lorraine, ⅛ of 8″ quiche . . . . 1 slice	1 slice	176	600	13	29	48	23.2	17.8	4.1	285
Spaghetti in tomato sauce with cheese:										
Canned . . . . 1 cup	1 cup	250	190	6	39	2	0.4	0.4	0.5	3
Home recipe . . . . 1 cup	1 cup	250	260	9	37	9	3.0	3.6	1.2	8
Spaghetti with meatballs and tomato sauce:										
Canned . . . . 1 cup	1 cup	250	260	12	29	10	2.4	3.9	3.1	23
Home recipe . . . . 1 cup	1 cup	248	330	19	39	12	3.9	4.4	2.2	89
Fast food entrees:										
Cheeseburger:										
Regular . . . . 1 sandwich	1 sandwich	112	300	15	28	15	7.3	5.6	1.0	44
4 oz. patty . . . . 1 sandwich	1 sandwich	194	525	30	40	31	15.1	12.2	1.4	104
Chicken, fried. See Poultry & poultry products.										
Enchilada . . . . 1 enchilada	1 enchilada	230	235	20	24	16	7.7	6.7	0.6	19
English muffin, egg, & bacon . . . . 1 sandwich	1 sandwich	138	360	18	31	18	8.0	8.0	0.7	213
Fish sandwich:										
Regular, with cheese . . . . 1 sandwich	1 sandwich	140	420	16	39	23	6.3	6.9	7.7	56
Large, no cheese. . . . . 1 sandwich	1 sandwich	170	470	18	41	27	6.3	8.7	9.5	91
Hamburger:										
Regular . . . . 1 sandwich	1 sandwich	98	245	12	28	11	4.4	5.3	0.5	32
4 oz. patty . . . . 1 sandwich	1 sandwich	174	445	25	38	21	7.1	11.7	0.6	71

Foods	Approximate Measure — Portion	Weight — Grams	Calories	Protein — Grams	Carbohydrate — Grams	Total Fat — Grams	Fats — Saturated — Grams	Fats — Mono-unsaturated — Grams	Fats — Poly-unsaturated — Grams	Cholesterol — Milligrams
Mixed Dishes and Fast Food										
Pizza, cheese, ⅛ of 15″ diam. pizza	1 slice	120	290	15	39	9	4.1	2.6	1.3	56
Roast beef sandwich	1 sandwich	150	345	22	34	13	3.5	6.9	1.8	55
Taco	1 taco	81	195	9	15	11	4.1	5.5	0.8	21
Poultry and Poultry Products										
Chicken:										
Fried, flesh, with skin:										
Batter dipped:										
½ breast, 5.6 oz with bones	4.9 oz	140	365	35	13	18	4.9	7.6	4.3	119
Drumstick, 3.4 oz with bones	2.5 oz	72	195	16	6	11	3.0	4.6	2.7	62
Flour coated:										
½ breast, 4.2 oz with bones	3.5 oz	98	220	31	2	9	2.4	3.4	1.9	87
Drumstick, 2.6 oz with bones	1.7 oz	49	120	13	1	7	1.8	2.7	1.6	44
Roasted, flesh only										
½ breast, 4.2 oz with bones & skin	3.0 oz	86	140	27	0	3	0.9	1.1	0.7	73
Drumstick, 2.9 oz with bones & skin	1.6 oz	44	75	12	0	2	0.7	0.8	0.6	41
Stewed, flesh only, chopped or diced	1 cup	140	250	38	0	9	2.6	3.3	2.2	116
Chicken liver, cooked	1 liver	20	30	5	tr	1	0.4	0.3	0.2	126

Food	Weight (g)								
Duck, roasted, flesh only . . . . ½ duck	221	445	52	0	25	9.2	8.2	3.2	197
Turkey, roasted, flesh only:									
Dark meat, piece, 2½ x 1⅝ x ¼''' . . . 4 pieces	85	160	24	0	6	2.1	1.4	1.8	72
Light meat, piece, 4 x 2 x ¼ . . . . . . 2 pieces	85	135	25	0	3	0.9	0.5	0.7	59
Light & dark meat:									
Chopped or diced . . . . .1 cup	140	240	41	0	7	2.3	1.4	2.0	106
Poultry food products:									
Chicken:									
Canned, boneless . . . . .5 oz	142	235	31	0	11	3.1	4.5	2.5	88
Frankfurter, 10/lb . . . . 1 frank	45	115	6	3	9	2.5	3.8	1.8	45
Roll, light, 1 oz/slice . . . . .2 slices	57	90	11	1	4	1.1	1.7	0.9	28
Turkey:									
Gravy & turkey, frozen. . . . . .5 oz	142	95	8	7	4	1.2	1.4	0.7	26
Ham, cured turkey thigh meat, 1 oz/slice . . . . 2 slices	57	75	11	tr	3	1.0	0.7	0.9	32
Loaf, breast meat, 8 slices/6 oz. pack . . . . 2 slices	42	45	10	0	1	0.2	0.2	0.1	17
Patties, breaded, battered, fried, 2.25 oz . . . . 1 patty	64	180	9	10	12	3.0	4.8	3.0	40
Roast, boneless, frozen, seasoned, light & dark meat, cooked . . . . . .3 oz	85	130	18	3	5	1.6	1.0	1.4	45

Soups, Sauces, and Gravies

Soups:

Canned, condensed:

Prepared with equal volume of milk:

Clam chowder,

Food									
New England. . . . . .1 cup	248	165	9	17	7	3.0	2.3	1.1	22
Cream of chicken . . . . .1 cup	248	190	7	15	11	4.6	4.5	1.6	27
Cream of mushroom . . . . .1 cup	248	205	6	15	14	5.1	3.0	4.6	20

227

Soups, Sauces, and Gravies continued

Foods	Approximate Measure	Weight	Calories	Protein	Carbohydrate	Total Fat	Fats			Cholesterol
							Saturated	Mono-unsaturated	Poly-unsaturated	
	Portion	Grams	Calories	Grams	Grams	Grams	Grams	Grams	Grams	Milligrams
Tomato....................1 cup		248	160	6	22	6	2.9	1.6	1.1	17
Prepared with equal volume of water:										
Bean with Bacon.............1 cup		253	170	8	23	6	1.5	2.2	1.8	3
Beef broth, bouillon, consomme.................1 cup		240	15	3	tr	1	0.3	0.2	tr	tr
Beef noodle................1 cup		244	85	5	9	3	1.1	1.2	0.5	5
Chicken noodle.............1 cup		241	75	4	9	2	0.7	1.1	0.6	7
Chicken rice...............1 cup		241	60	4	7	2	0.5	0.9	0.4	7
Clam chowder, Manhattan......1 cup		244	80	4	12	2	0.4	0.4	1.3	2
Cream of chicken............1 cup		244	115	3	9	7	2.1	3.3	1.5	10
Cream of mushroom..........1 cup		244	130	2	9	9	2.4	1.7	4.2	2
Minestrone.................1 cup		241	80	4	11	3	0.6	0.7	1.1	2
Pea, green.................1 cup		250	165	9	27	3	1.4	1.0	0.4	0
Tomato....................1 cup		244	85	2	17	2	0.4	0.4	1.0	0
Vegetable beef.............1 cup		244	80	6	10	2	0.9	0.8	0.1	5
Vegetarian.................1 cup		241	70	2	12	2	0.3	0.8	0.7	0
Dehydrated:										
Unprepared:										
Bouillon..................1 pkt		6	15	1	1	1	0.3	0.2	tr	1
Onion....................1 pkt		7	20	1	4	tr	0.1	0.2	tr	tr
Prepared with 6 oz water:										
Chicken noodle.............1 pkt		188	40	2	6	1	0.2	0.4	0.3	6
Onion....................1 pkt		184	20	1	4	tr	0.1	0.2	0.1	4
Tomato vegetable...........1 pkt		189	40	1	8	1	0.3	0.2	0.1	8

Sauces:

From dry mix:

Food	Measure								
Cheese, prepared with milk	1 cup	279	305	16	17	9.3	5.3	1.6	23
Hollandaise, prepared with water	1 cup	259	240	5	20	11.6	5.9	0.9	14
White sauce, prepared with milk	1 cup	264	240	10	13	6.4	4.7	1.7	21

From home recipe:

Food	Measure								
White sauce, medium	1 cup	250	395	10	30	9.1	11.9	7.2	24

Ready to serve:

Food	Measure								
Barbecue	1 Tbs	16	10	tr	tr	tr	0.1	0.1	2
Soy	1 Tbs	18	10	2	0	0.0	0.0	0.0	2

Gravies:

Canned:

Food	Measure								
Beef	1 cup	233	125	9	5	2.7	2.3	0.2	11
Chicken	1 cup	238	190	5	14	3.4	6.1	3.6	13
Mushroom	1 cup	238	120	3	6	1.0	2.8	2.4	13

From dry mix:

Food	Measure								
Brown	1 cup	261	80	3	2	0.9	0.8	0.1	14
Chicken	1 cup	260	85	3	2	0.5	0.9	0.4	14

Sugars and Sweets

Candy:

Food	Measure								
Caramels, plain or chocolate	1 oz	28	115	1	3	2.2	0.3	0.1	22

Chocolate:

Food	Measure								
Milk, plain	1 oz	28	145	2	9	5.4	3.0	0.3	16
Milk, with almonds	1 oz	28	150	3	10	4.8	4.1	0.7	15
Milk, with peanuts	1 oz	28	155	4	11	4.2	3.5	1.5	13
Milk, with rice cereal	1 oz	28	140	2	7	4.4	2.5	0.2	18

Sugars and Sweets

	Fats		

Foods	Approximate Measure Portion	Weight Grams	Calories Calories	Protein Grams	Carbohydrate Grams	Total Fat Grams	Saturated Grams	Mono-unsaturated Grams	Poly-unsaturated Grams	Cholesterol Milligrams
Semisweet, small pieces, 60/oz ....1 cup	1 cup	170	860	7	97	61	36.2	19.9	1.9	96
Sweet (dark).................	1 oz	28	150	1	16	10	5.9	3.3	0.3	16
Fondant, uncoated (mints, candy corn, other)	1 oz	28	105	tr	27	0	0.0	0.0	0.0	27
Fudge, chocolate, plain.	1 oz	28	115	1	21	3	2.1	1.0	0.1	21
Gum drops.................	1 oz	28	100	tr	25	tr	tr	tr	0.1	25
Hard..................	1 oz	28	110	0	28	0	0.0	tr	0.0	0
Jelly beans..............	1 oz	28	105	tr	26	tr	tr	tr	0.1	0
Marshmallows.............	1 oz	28	90	1	23	0	0.0	0.0	0.0	0
Custard, baked	1 cup	265	305	14	29	15	6.8	5.4	0.7	278
Gelatin dessert prepared with gelatin powder & water	½ cup	120	70	2	17	0	0.0	0.0	0.0	0
Honey......................	1 cup	339	1,030	1	279	0	0.0	0.0	0.0	0
	1 Tbs	21	65	tr	17	0	0.0	0.0	0.0	0
Jams & preserves	1 Tbs	20	55	tr	14	tr	0.0	tr	tr	0
	1 pkt	14	40	tr	10	tr	0.0	tr	tr	0
Jellies....................	1 Tbs	18	50	tr	13	tr	tr	tr	tr	0
	1 pkt	14	40	tr	10	tr	tr	tr	tr	0
Popsicle, 3-fl-oz.............	1 pop	95	70	0	18	0	0.0	0.0	0.0	0
Puddings: Canned:										
Chocolate	5 oz	142	205	3	30	11	9.5	0.5	0.1	1
Tapioca	5 oz	142	160	3	28	5	4.8	tr	tr	tr
Vanilla................	5 oz	142	220	2	33	10	9.5	0.2	0.1	1

Dry mix, prepared with whole milk:

Chocolate:									
Instant . . . . ½ cup	130	155	4	27	4	2.3	1.1	0.2	14
Regular, cooked . . . . ½ cup	130	150	4	25	4	2.4	1.1	0.1	15
Rice . . . . ½ cup	132	155	4	27	4	2.3	1.1	0.1	15
Tapioca . . . . ½ cup	130	145	4	25	4	2.3	1.1	0.1	15
Vanilla:									
Instant . . . . ½ cup	130	150	4	27	4	2.2	1.1	0.2	15
Regular . . . . ½ cup	130	145	4	25	4	2.3	1.0	0.1	15
Sugars:									
Brown, pressed down . . . . 1 cup	220	820	0	212	0	0.0	0.0	0.0	0
White:									
Granulated . . . . 1 cup	200	770	0	199	0	0.0	0.0	0.0	0
1 Tbs	12	45	0	12	0	0.0	0.0	0.0	0
1 pkt	6	25	0	6	0	0.0	0.0	0.0	0
Powdered, sifted, spooned into cup . . . . 1 cup	100	385	0	100	0	0.0	0.0	0.0	0
Syrups:									
Chocolate-flavored syrup or topping:									
Thin type . . . . 2 Tbs	38	85	1	22	tr	0.2	0.1	0.1	0
Fudge type . . . . 2 Tbs	38	125	2	21	5	3.1	1.7	0.2	0
Molasses, cane, blackstrap . . . . 2 Tbs	40	85	0	22	0	0.0	0.0	0.0	0
Table syrup, corn & maple . . . . 2 Tbs	42	122	0	32	0	0.0	0.0	0.0	0

Vegetable and Vegetable Products

Alfalfa seed, sprouted . . . . 1 cup	33	10	1	1	tr	tr	tr	0.1	0
Artichokes, cooked . . . . 1 art	120	55	3	12	tr	tr	tr	0.1	0

Vegetable and Vegetables Products continued

Foods	Approximate Measure (Portion)	Weight (Grams)	Calories	Protein (Grams)	Carbohydrate (Grams)	Total Fat (Grams)	Saturated (Grams)	Mono-unsaturated (Grams)	Poly-unsaturated (Grams)	Cholesterol (Milligrams)
Asparagus, green:										
Cooked, drained:										
From raw:										
Cuts & tips............1 cup		180	45	5	8	1	0.1	tr	0.2	0
Spears, ½" diam. at base.....4 spears		60	15	2	3	tr	tr	tr	0.1	0
From frozen:										
Cuts & tips............1 cup		180	50	5	9	1	0.2	tr	0.3	0
Spears, ½" diam. at base.....4 spears		60	15	2	3	tr	0.1	tr	0.1	0
Canned, spears, ½" diam. at base.......4 spears		80	10	1	2	tr	tr	tr	0.1	0
Bamboo shoots, canned, drained......1 cup		131	25	2	4	1	0.1	tr	0.2	0
Beans:										
Lima, immature seeds, frozen, cooked, drained:										
Thick-seeded types........1 cup		170	170	10	32	1	0.1	tr	0.3	0
Thin-seeded types.........1 cup		180	190	12	35	1	0.1	tr	0.3	0
Snap:										
Cooked, drained:										
From raw, cut &										
French style.........1 cup		125	45	2	10	tr	0.1	tr	0.2	0
Frozen, cut..........1 cup		135	35	2	8	tr	tr	tr	0.1	0
Canned, drained.........cup		135	25	2	6	tr	tr	tr	0.1	0
Bean sprouts, mung:										
Raw...............1 cup		104	30	3	6	tr	tr	tr	0.1	0
Cooked, drained........1 cup		124	25	3	5	tr	tr	tr	tr	0

Beets:									
Cooked, drained:									
Diced or sliced............1 cup	170	55	2	11	tr	tr	tr	tr	0
Whole, 2″ diam..........2 beets	100	30	1	7	tr	tr	tr	tr	0
Canned, drained, diced									
or sliced ....1 cup	170	55	2	12	tr	tr	tr	0.1	0
Beet greens, leaves & stems,									
cooked, drained ....1 cup	144	40	4	8	tr	tr	0.1	0.1	0
Black-eyed peas, immature									
seed, cooked:									
From raw ....1 cup	165	180	13	30	1	0.3	0.1	0.6	0
From frozen ....1 cup	170	225	14	40	1	0.3	0.1	0.5	0
Broccoli:									
Raw ....1 spear	151	40	4	8	1	0.1	tr	0.3	0
Cooked:									
From raw:									
Spear, medium ....1 spear	180	50	5	10	1	0.1	tr	0.2	0
Cut in ½‴ pieces ....1 cup	155	45	5	9	tr	0.1	tr	0.2	0
From frozen:									
Piece, 4–5″ long............1 piece	30	10	1	2	tr	tr	tr	tr	0
Chopped............1 cup	185	50	6	10	tr	tr	tr	0.1	0
Brussels sprouts, cooked, drained:									
From raw, 7–8 sprouts ....1 cup	155	60	4	13	1	0.2	0.1	0.4	0
From frozen............1 cup	155	65	6	13	1	0.1	tr	0.3	0
Cabbage:									
Raw, coarsely shredded or sliced ....1 cup	70	15	1	4	tr	tr	tr	0.1	0
Cooked, drained............1 cup	150	30	1	7	tr	tr	tr	0.2	0
Cabbage, Chinese:									
Pak-choi, cooked............1 cup	170	20	3	3	tr	tr	tr	0.1	0
Pe-tsai, raw, 1″............1 cup	76	10	1	2	tr	tr	tr	0.1	0

233

Vegetable and Vegetable Products continued

Foods	Approximate Measure Portion	Weight Grams	Calories	Protein Grams	Carbohydrate Grams	Total Fat Grams	Saturated Grams	Mono-unsaturated Grams	Poly-unsaturated Grams	Cholesterol Milligrams
Cabbage, red, raw, coarsely shredded or sliced ...1 cup	70	20	1	4	tr	tr	tr	0.1	0	
Cabbage, savoy, raw, coarsely shredded...1 cup	70	20	1	4	tr	tr	tr	tr	0	
Carrots:										
Raw, scraped:										
Whole, 7½ x 1⅛...1 carrot	72	30	1	7	tr	tr	tr	0.1	0	
Grated...1 cup	110	45	1	11	tr	tr	tr	0.1	0	
Cooked, sliced:										
From raw...1 cup	156	70	2	16	tr	0.1	tr	0.1	0	
From frozen...1 cup	146	55	2	12	tr	tr	tr	0.1	0	
Canned, sliced...1 cup	146	35	1	8	tr	0.1	tr	0.1	0	
Cauliflower:										
Raw (flowerets)...1 cup	100	25	2	5	tr	tr	tr	0.1	0	
Cooked, drained:										
From raw, flowerets...1 cup	125	30	2	6	tr	tr	tr	0.1	0	
Frozen, flowerets...1 cup	180	35	3	7	tr	0.1	tr	0.2	0	
Celery, pascal type, raw:										
Stalk, large outer, 8 x 1½" at root end...1 stalk	40	5	tr	1	tr	tr	tr	tr	0	
Diced...1 cup	120	20	1	4	tr	tr	tr	0.1	0	
Collards, cooked, drained:										
From raw, leaves without stems...1 cup	190	25	2	5	tr	0.1	tr	0.2	0	
From frozen...1 cup	170	60	5	12	1	0.1	0.1	0.4	0	

Corn, sweet:									
Cooked, drained:									
From raw, ear 5 x 2" ....1 ear	77	85	3	19	1	0.2	0.3	0.5	0
From frozen:									
Ear 3½" long ....1 ear	63	60	2	14	tr	0.1	0.1	0.2	0
Kernels ....1 cup	165	135	5	34	tr	tr	tr	0.1	0
Canned:									
Cream style ....1 cup	256	185	4	46	1	0.2	0.3	0.5	0
Whole kernel ....1 cup	210	165	5	41	1	0.2	0.3	0.5	0
Cucumber, with peel, slices, ⅛" thick ....6 lg or 8 sm slices	28	5	tr	1	tr	tr	tr	tr	0
Dandelion greens, cooked, drained ....1 cup	105	35	2	7	1	0.1	tr	0.3	0
Eggplant, cooked ....1 cup	96	25	1	6	tr	tr	tr	0.1	0
Endive, curly, raw, small pieces .....1 cup	50	10	1	2	tr	tr	tr	tr	0
Jerusalem-artichoke, raw, sliced ......1 cup	150	115	3	26	tr	0.0	tr	tr	0
Kale, cooked, drained:									
From raw, chopped ....1 cup	130	40	2	7	1	0.1	tr	0.3	0
From frozen ....1 cup	130	40	4	7	1	0.1	tr	0.3	0
Kohlrabi, thickened bulb-like stems, cooked, diced ....1 cup	165	50	3	11	tr	tr	tr	0.1	0
Lettuce, raw:									
Butterhead, as Boston:									
Head, 5" diam. .... 1 head	163	20	2	4	tr	tr	tr	0.2	0
Leaves.............1 outer or 2 inner	15	tr	tr	tr	tr	tr	tr	tr	0
Crisphead, as iceberg:									
Head, 6" diam. .... 1 head	539	70	5	11	1	0.1	tr	0.5	0
Wedge, ¼ of head.............1 wedge	135	20	1	3	tr	tr	tr	0.1	0
Pieces, chopped ....1 cup	55	5	1	1	tr	tr	tr	0.1	0

Vegetable and Vegetable Products continued

Foods	Approximate Measure	Weight	Calories	Protein	Carbohydrate	Total Fat	Fats Saturated	Mono-unsaturated	Poly-unsaturated	Cholesterol
	Portion	Grams	Calories	Grams	Grams	Grams	Grams	Grams	Grams	Milligrams
Looseleaf, bunching varieties such as romaine, chopped or shredded ....1 cup		56	10	1	2	tr	tr	tr	0.1	0
Mushrooms:										
Raw, sliced......................1 cup		70	20	1	3	tr	tr	tr	0.1	0
Cooked, drained...............1 cup		156	40	3	8	1	0.1	tr	0.3	0
Canned, drained...............1 cup		156	35	3	8	tr	0.1	tr	0.2	0
Mustard greens, without stems & midribs, cooked ....1 cup		140	20	3	3	tr	tr	0.2	0.1	0
Okra pods, cooked .... 8 pods		85	25	2	6	tr	tr	tr	tr	0
Onions:										
Raw:										
Chopped........................1 cup		160	55	2	12	tr	0.1	0.1	0.2	0
Sliced...........................1 cup		115	40	1	8	tr	0.1	tr	0.1	0
Cooked, whole or sliced, drained....1 cup		210	60	2	13	tr	0.1	tr	0.1	0
Onions, spring, raw, bulb, ⅜" diam. & white portion of top ....6 onions		30	10	1	2	tr	tr	tr	tr	0
Onion rings, breaded, par-fried, frozen .... 2 rings		20	80	1	8	5	1.7	2.2	1.0	0
Parsley:										
Raw .... 10 sprigs		10	5	tr	1	tr	tr	tr	tr	0
Freeze-dried ....1 Tbs		0.4	tr	tr	tr	tr	tr	tr	tr	0
Parsnips, cooked..............1 cup		156	125	2	30	tr	0.1	0.2	0.1	0
Peas, edible pod, cooked......1 cup		160	65	5	11	tr	0.1	tr	0.2	0

Food	Measure									
Peas, green:										
Canned, drained	1 cup	170	115	8	21	1	0.1	0.1	0.3	0
Frozen, cooked	1 cup	160	125	8	23	tr	0.1	tr	0.2	0
Peppers:										
Hot chili, raw	1 pepper	45	20	1	4	tr	tr	tr	tr	0
Sweet (5/lb):										
Raw	1 pepper	74	20	1	4	tr	tr	tr	0.2	0
Cooked	1 pepper	73	15	tr	3	tr	tr	tr	0.1	0
Potatoes, cooked:										
Baked (2/lb):										
With skin	1 potato	202	220	5	51	tr	0.1	tr	0.1	0
Flesh only	1 potato	156	145	3	34	tr	tr	tr	0.1	0
Boiled (3/lb):										
Peeled after	1 potato	136	120	3	27	tr	tr	tr	0.1	0
Peeled before	1 potato	135	115	2	27	tr	tr	tr	0.1	0
French fried, frozen:										
Oven heated	10 strips	50	110	2	17	4	2.1	1.8	0.3	0
Fried in veg. oil	10 strips	50	160	2	20	8	2.5	1.6	3.8	0
Potato products, prepared:										
Au gratin:										
From dry mix	1 cup	245	230	6	31	10	6.3	2.9	0.3	12
From home mix	1 cup	245	325	12	28	19	11.6	5.3	0.7	56
Hashed brown, from frozen	1 cup	156	340	5	44	18	7.0	8.0	2.1	0
Mashed:										
From home recipe:										
Milk added	1 cup	210	160	4	37	1	0.7	0.3	0.1	4
Milk & margarine	1 cup	210	225	4	35	9	2.2	3.7	2.5	4
From dehydrated flakes (without milk), water, milk, butter & salt added	1 cup	210	235	4	32	12	7.2	3.3	0.5	29

Foods	Approximate Measure Portion	Weight Grams	Calories Calories	Protein Grams	Carbohydrate Grams	Total Fat Grams	Fats Saturated Grams	Fats Mono-unsaturated Grams	Fats Poly-unsaturated Grams	Cholesterol Milligrams
Vegetable and Vegetable Products continued										
Potato salad, made with										
mayonnaise ...1 cup	250	360	7	28	21	3.6	6.2	9.3	170
Scalloped:										
From dry mix...1 cup	245	230	5	31	11	6.5	3.0	0.5	27
From home recipe ...1 cup	245	210	7	26	9	5.5	2.5	0.4	29
Potato chips...10 chips	20	105	1	10	7	1.8	1.2	3.6	0
Pumpkin:										
Cooked from raw ...1 cup	245	50	2	12	tr	0.1	tr	tr	0
Canned...1 cup	245	85	3	20	1	0.4	0.1	tr	0
Radishes, raw ...4 radishes	18	5	tr	1	tr	tr	tr	tr	0
Sauerkraut, canned, solid										
and liquid...1 cup	236	45	2	10	tr	0.1	tr	0.1	0
Seaweed:										
Kelp, raw ...1 oz	28	10	tr	3	tr	0.1	tr	tr	0
Spirulina ...1 oz	28	80	16	7	2	0.8	0.2	0.6	0
Spinach:										
Raw, chopped...1 cup	55	10	2	2	tr	tr	tr	0.1	0
Cooked, drained:										
From raw ...1 cup	180	40	5	7	tr	0.1	tr	0.2	0
From frozen...1 cup	190	55	6	10	tr	0.1	tr	0.2	0
Canned, drained...1 cup	214	50	6	7	1	0.2	tr	0.4	0
Spinach souffle ...1 cup	136	220	11	3	18	7.1	6.8	3.1	184
Squash, cooked:										
Summer, sliced ...1 cup	180	35	2	3	1	0.1	tr	0.2	0
Winter, baked, cubed ...1 cup	205	80	2	18	1	0.3	0.1	0.5	0

Sweet potatoes:
Cooked (raw, 5 x 2"):

Food	Measure									
Baked, then peeled	1 potato	114	115	2	28	tr	tr	tr	0.1	0
Boiled, peeled	1 potato	151	160	2	37	tr	0.1	tr	0.2	0
Candied, 2½ x 2"	1 piece	105	145	1	29	3	1.4	0.7	0.2	8
Canned:										
Solid pack, mashed	1 cup	255	260	5	59	1	0.1	tr	0.2	0
Pieces, 2¾ x 1"	1 piece	40	35	1	8	tr	tr	tr	tr	0
Tomatoes:										
Raw, 2⅗" diam.	1 tomato	123	25	1	5	tr	tr	tr	0.1	0
Canned, solids & lq	1 cup	240	50	2	10	1	0.1	0.1	0.2	0
Tomato juice, canned	1 cup	244	40	2	10	tr	tr	tr	0.1	0
Tomato products, canned:										
Paste	1 cup	262	220	10	49	2	0.3	0.4	0.9	0
Puree	1 cup	250	105	4	25	tr	tr	tr	0.1	0
Sauce	1 cup	245	75	3	18	tr	0.1	0.1	0.2	0
Turnips, cooked	1 cup	156	30	1	8	tr	tr	tr	0.1	0
Turnip greens, cooked, drained:										
From raw	1 cup	144	30	2	6	tr	0.1	tr	0.1	0
From frozen, chopped	1 cup	164	50	5	8	1	0.2	tr	0.3	0
Vegetable juice cocktail, canned	1 cup	242	45	2	11	tr	tr	tr	0.1	0
Vegetables, mixed:										
Canned, drained	1 cup	163	75	4	15	tr	0.1	tr	0.2	0
Frozen, cooked	1 cup	182	105	5	24	tr	0.1	tr	0.1	0
Waterchestnuts	1 cup	140	70	1	17	tr	tr	tr	tr	0

Foods	Approximate Measure Portion	Weight Grams	Calories Calories	Protein Grams	Carbohydrate Grams	Total Fat Grams	Fats			Cholesterol Milligrams
							Saturated Grams	Mono-unsaturated Grams	Poly-unsaturated Grams	
Miscellaneous										
Baking powders for home use:										
Sodium aluminum sulfate:										
With monocalcium phosphate										
monohydrate... 1 tsp	3	5	tr	1	0	0.0	0.0	0.0	0
With monocalcium phosphate										
monohydrate, calcium sulfate ... 1 tsp	2.9	5	tr	1	0	0.0	0.0	0.0	0
Straight phosphate... 1 tsp	3.8	5	tr	1	0	0.0	0.0	0.0	0
Low sodium... 1 tsp	4.3	5	tr	1	0	0.0	0.0	0.0	0
Catsup... 1 cup	273	290	5	69	1	0.2	0.2	0.4	0
1 Tbs	15	15	tr	4	tr	tr	tr	tr	0
Celery seed... 1 tsp	2	10	tr	1	1	tr	0.3	0.1	0
Chili powder... 1 tsp	2.6	10	tr	1	tr	0.1	0.1	0.2	0
Chocolate:										
Bitter or baking... 1 oz	28	145	3	8	15	9.0	4.9	0.5	0
Semisweet, see Candy										
Cinnamon... 1 tsp	2.3	5	tr	2	tr	tr	tr	tr	0
Curry powder... 1 tsp	2	5	tr	1	tr	—	—	—	0
Garlic powder... 1 tsp	2.8	10	tr	2	tr	tr	tr	tr	0
Gelatin, dry... 1 pkt	7	25	6	0	tr	tr	tr	tr	0
Mustard, prepared,... 1 tsp	5	5	tr	tr	tr	tr	0.2	tr	0
Olives, canned:										
Green... 4 med or 3 x-lg	13	15	tr	tr	2	0.2	1.2	0.1	0
Ripe, Mission... 3 sm or 2 lg	9	15	tr	tr	2	0.3	1.3	0.2	0

Onion powder	1 tsp	2.1	5	tr	2	tr	tr	tr	tr	0
Oregano	1 tsp	1.5	5	tr	1	tr	tr	tr	0.1	0
Paprika	1 tsp	2.1	5	tr	1	tr	tr	tr	0.2	0
Pepper black	1 tsp	2.1	5	tr	1	tr	tr	tr	tr	0
Pickles, cucumber:										
Dill, 3¾ x 1¼" ....1 pickle		65	5	tr	1	tr	tr	tr	0.1	0
Fresh pack, slices 1½ x ¼" ...2 slices		15	10	tr	3	tr	tr	tr	tr	0
Sweet gherkin, small ......1 pickle		15	20	tr	5	tr	tr	tr	tr	0
Relish, finely chopped, sweet ......1 Tbs		15	20	tr	5	tr	tr	tr	tr	0
Salt	1 tsp	5.5	0	0	0	0	0.0	0.0	0.0	0
Vinegar, cider	1 Tbs	15	tr	tr	1	tr	0.0	0.0	0.0	0
Yeast:										
Baker's, dry active	1 pkg	7	20	3	3	tr	tr	tr	tr	0
Brewer's dry	1 Tbs	8	25	3	3	tr	tr	tr	0.0	0

A la cart

BIBLIOGRAPHY

Anderson, James W., M.D. "Dietary Fiber and Heart Disease: Current Management Concepts and Recommendations." Topics In Clinical Nutrition, April, 1988

Boekeloo, Bradley O., ScM. et al. "Cholesterol Management in Patients Hospitalized for Coronary Heart Disease." American Journal of Preventive Medicine, 1988

Castelli, William P., M.D., et al. "Incidence of Coronary Heart Disease and Lipoprotein Cholesterol Levels—The Framingham Study." Journal of the American Medical Association, Vol. 256, no. 20, November 28, 1986

Castelli, William P., M.D. "Cardiovascular Disease In Women." American Journal of Obstetrics and Gynecology, June 1988

"Choice of Cholesterol-Lowering Drugs." The Medical Letter, New Rochelle, N.Y., September 9, 1988

"Cholesterol: The Numbers." Harvard Medical School Health Letter, March, 5, 1989

Cooper, Kenneth H., M.D., M.P.H. Controlling Cholesterol, Bantam Books, New York, N.Y. 1988

Cotton, Paul. "Targeting the Individual Cholesterol." Medical World News, November, 14, 1988

DeBakey, Michael E., et al. The Living Heart Diet. New York: Raven Press/Simon and Schuster, 1984

Eating to Lower Your High Blood Cholesterol. U.S. Department of Health and Human Services, September 1987

Earnest, Barbara & Schlesinger, Sarah. The Low-Cholesterol Oat Plan: A Revolutionary Oat Bran Cookbook That Can Save Your Life. Hearst Books, New York, 1988

Farrand, Marilyn E., MS,RD. "National Cholesterol Education Program Guidelines: New Opportunities and Challenges For Dietitians." Topics In Clinical Nutrition, 1988

"Facts About Blood Cholesterol." U.S. Department of Health and Human Services, National Institutes of Health, 1987

"Fact Sheet On Heart Attack, Stroke and Risk Factors." American Heart Association, 1988

Fisher, Hans, PhD. & Boe, Eugene. The Rutgers Guide to Lowering Your Cholesterol: A Common-Sense Approach. Warner Books, 1985

"Give Diet a Chance in Lowering Cholesterol Levels." Archives Internal Medicine, May, 1988

Gold, Kurt V. and Davidson, Dennis M., M.D. "Oat Bran As A Cholesterol-Reducing Dietary Adjunct In A Young, Healthy Population." The Western Journal of Medicine, March, 1988

Grundy, Scott M., M.D., PhD. et al. "Comparison of Monounsaturated Fatty Acids and Carbohydrates For Reducing Raised Levels of Plasma Cholesterol in Man." American Journal Clinical Nutrition, 1988

Healthy Heart Handbook For Women. U.S. Department of Health and Human Services, 1987

Kowalski, Robert E. Eight Week Cholesterol Cure. Harper & Row, New York, 1987

Lecos, Chris W. Do Your Heart A Favor. Department of Health and Human Services, 1988

Miller, Roger W., "The Cholesterol Connection." Department of Health and Human Services, 1986

"Olive-Oil-Enriched Diet: Effect On Serum Lipoprotein Levels and Biliary Cholesterol Saturation." American Journal of Clinical Nutrition, 1988

"Recommendations For Treatment of Hyperlipidemia in Adults." American Heart Association, 1986

"Report of the Expert Panel on Detection, Evaluation, and Treatment of High Blood Cholesterol in Adults." U.S. Department of Health and Human Services, January, 1989

So You Have High Blood Cholesterol . . . U.S. Department of Health and Human Services, September, 1987

Stone, Neil J., M.D., VanHorn, Linda V., PhD. RD. "Controlling Cholesterol Levels Through Diet." Postgraduate Medicine, June, 1988

Ulene, Art. Count Down On Cholesterol, Knopf, New York, N.Y. 1989

GLOSSARY

Aerobic exercise—endurance type of physical activity which requires only a modest increase in oxygen intake, increases the heart rate and produces beneficial changes in the respiratory and circulatory systems. Found to be beneficial in raising the "good" HDL cholesterol.

Angina—a pain usually in the chest resulting from a reversible condition in which the heart muscle is not receiving sufficient blood supply. Usually this is caused by the coronary arteries being blocked with cholesterol and fatty deposits, limiting the blood supply which is necessary for the heart to function properly. The pain may also occur in the arm, shoulder, back or neck as a pressure, burning or squeezing. It typically is provoked by effort or emotional stress but can occur spontaneously.

Angiography—test in which a catheter is inserted into an arm or groin artery and threaded through the blood vessels to the heart. Opaque dye is then injected directly into the coronary arteries and X-ray motion pictures of the coronary arteries are taken. This gives a clear picture of the severity of the coronary artery obstruction.

Aorta—the large artery that receives blood from the left ventricle of the heart and distributes it to the body.

Arteriography—test in which a dye is injected into the bloodstream and then x-ray pictures are taken to see if the arteries are damaged.

Arteriosclerosis—commonly called hardening of the arteries. This includes a variety of conditions that cause the artery walls to thicken and lose elasticity.

Artery—any one of a series of blood vessels that carry blood from the heart to all parts of the body. Arteries have thick, elastic walls that expand as blood flows through them and end in small branches called arterioles, which in turn branch to form smaller tubes called capillaries.

Atherosclerosis—type of "hardening of the arteries" in which cholesterol, fat and other blood components build up on the inner lining of arteries. As atherosclerosis progresses, the arteries to the heart, brain and other areas of the body may narrow so that oxygen-rich blood and nutrient have difficulty reaching the cells of the body.

Bile acid sequestrant—type of cholesterol-lowering medication, including cholestyramine and colestipol, that binds with cholesterol-containing bile acids in the intestine and prevents the reabsorption of cholesterol into the body and blood vessels.

Blood cholesterol—cholesterol that is manufactured in the liver and absorbed from the food you eat and is carried in the blood for use by the body.

Blood clot—a jelly-like mass of blood tissue formed by the clotting factors in the blood. Clots can form inside an artery whose walls are damaged by atherosclerotic buildup and can cause a heart attack or stroke.

Blood pressure—the force or pressure exerted by the heart in pumping blood through the arteries.

Bran—outer tough coating of grains, such as oats, rye, and wheat, that is separated in the refining process but is included in whole- grain products. It may also be added to cereals and other grain products. Oat and rice bran have been found to be beneficial in lowering blood cholesterol.

Calorie—unit of measure of the amount of energy a food provides to the body. Food energy comes from three sources: fats, carbohydrates and proteins. Carbohydrates and proteins provide 4 calories per gram, fats 9 calories per gram, and alcohol 7 calories per grams but no nutrients.

Capillaries—minute blood vessels with walls one cell thick which connect the smallest arteries (arterioles) with the smallest veins (venules). They carry oxygen and nutrients to the tissues.

Carbohydrates—one of the three basic food materials containing only carbon, hydrogen and oxygen. They are the foods comprised of starches, sugars and fiber such as whole grains, vegetables and fruits. Carbohydrates provide four calories per gram. There are two kinds of carbohydrates in the natural form and they come packaged together in whole grains, vegetables and fruits.

1. Complex carbohydrates (starches and fibers)—foods high in starches and fibers are whole grain products and vegetables.
2. Simple carbohydrates (sugars)—foods high in sugars are fruits. When carbohydrates are refined (processed), the end products such as white flour, sugar and polished rice, are usually low in vitamins, minerals and fiber. It is the refined carbohydrates that are usually used to make cookies, cakes, pies, candies, etc. which do not contain much food value.

Cardiac—pertaining to the heart.

Cardiovascular—pertaining to the heart and blood vessels.

Carotid artery—major artery in the neck taking blood to the brain.

Cell—basic structural and functional unit of the body. Every tissue and organ is composed of cells each of which is to some extent a self-contained unit, but relies on others for its continued existence.

Cerebral embolism—blood clot that has formed in one part of the body and then been carried by the bloodstream to the brain, where it becomes lodged in an artery, can cause a stroke.

Cerebral thrombosis—formation of a blood clot in an artery that supplies blood to part of the brain.

Cholesterol—fat like substance found in animal tissue, present only in foods from animal sources such as dairy products, meat, fish, poultry, egg yolks and animal fats. It is necessary for the production of Vitamin D on the surface of the skin, for making various hormones including the sex hormones. The body can make all the cholesterol it needs. It is essential to body functions.

Circulatory system—the heart pumping the blood to the arteries to all parts of the body and the blood returning to the heart through the veins. The pathway of the blood is from the heart → aorta → arteries → arterioles→ capillaries → venules → veins → vena cava → heart.

Coronary arteries—two arteries branching directly from the aorta, spread over the heart to supply the heart muscle with blood.

Coronary heart disease—damage to the heart muscle due to insufficient blood flow through the coronary arteries.

Dietary cholesterol—cholesterol that is in the foods we eat, found only in foods of animal origin.

Essential fatty acids—fatty acids that the body cannot make and which must be supplied by the diet.

Fat—constituent of most foods of plant and animal origin. A major source of energy, also plays a key role as carrier of fat-soluble vitamins (A, D, E, K). Two types of fat are:
  1. Saturated—solid at room temperature. Found in greatest amounts in foods from animals such as meat, poultry, and whole-milk products and some vegetable oils such as coconut, palm, palm kernel and cocoa butter. Saturated fat raises blood cholesterol more than anything else you eat.
  2. Unsaturated—liquid at room temperature. Found primarily in vegetable and fish oils. There are two types:
      1) Polyunsaturated fats—found in safflower oil, soybean oil, sesame oil, sunflower oil, corn oil, nuts, seeds. These fats lower both the "bad" LDLs and the "good" HDLs.
      2) Monounsaturated fats—found in canola (rapeseed) oil and olive oil. These fats lower only the "bad" LDLs which is what you want.

Fiber—indigestible carbohydrate component of plant food. Foods high in fiber include whole grain products, whole fruits and vegetables and legumes.
- Soluble fiber—found in oats, oat bran, rice bran barley and legumes (dried beans, peas, lentils), psyllium seeds and some fruits such as grapefruit and apple and some vegetables such as carrots. Helpful in lowering high blood cholesterol.
- Insoluble fiber—found in whole grains, wheat and corn bran, dry whole grain cereals, some fruits and vegetables. Does not help lower cholesterol but does helps speed the digested food through the bowel, helpful in preventing constipation, hemorrhoids and diverticulosis.

Genes—the carriers of physical, chemical and psychological traits from parents to offspring, generation to generation.

Genetics—the branch of biology dealing with heredity, which studies the way genes operate and the way they are transmitted from parent to offspring.

Gram (g or gm)—unit of weight, about 28 grams in one ounce and 453.6 grams in one pound.

Heart attack—death of, or damage to part of the heart muscle due to an insufficient blood supply.

Heredity—the genetic transfer of a quality or trait from parent to off-spring.

High density lipoproteins (HDL)—see lipoproteins.

Hydrogenation—chemical process adding hydrogen to liquid vegetable oils (unsaturated fat) which makes them into a solid fat (saturated). Many commercial food products contain hydrogenated vegetable oil because it improves the shelf life of the product.

Hypercholesterolemia—elevation of the cholesterol concentration in the blood.

Hyperlipidemia—abnormally high concentration of fats (lipids) in the blood; usually relates to blood cholesterol and/or triglycerides.

Lipids—another name for fats, including cholesterol, triglycerides and phospholipids, substances that provide energy to the body and contribute to cell structure. They are insoluble in blood.

Lipoprotein—protein coated packages that carry all the lipids, including cholesterol and triglycerides, through the blood and making them soluble in blood. They are classified according to their density.
- High density lipoproteins (HDLs)—contain a small amount of cholesterol and carry it away from body cells and tissues to the liver for excretion from the body; therefore called "good" cholesterol. Low levels of HDLs are associated with coronary heart disease so you want a high level of HDLs for protection.

- Low density lipoproteins (LDLs)—contain the largest amount of cholesterol in the blood; are responsible for depositing cholesterol in the artery walls. High levels of LDLs are associated with atherosclerosis and coronary heart disease and are referred to as "bad" cholesterol.
- Very low density lipoprotein—transports triglycerides through the blood.

Low density lipoproteins (LDL)—see lipoprotein.

Monounsaturated fats—see fats.

Milligram (mg)—measure of weight; $\frac{1}{1000}$ of a gram.

Myocardial infarction—another term for heart attack or coronary thrombosis. It refers to the death of part of the heart muscle (myocardium) from lack of blood supply due usually to a clot blocking a coronary artery.

Niacin—a B vitamin; when used under a physician's guidance it is considered a cholesterol-lowering medication.

Plaque—deposit of fatty (and other) materials and cholesterol on the inner surface of an artery that may narrow or block the interior diameter of the artery. It is the leading cause of heart attack.

Polyunsaturated fats—see fats

Protein—one of the three main food components; essential for tissue building and repair. Found primarily in meats, dairy products, grains and legumes. Protein provides 4 calories per gram, the same as carbohydrates but less than half the amount of fat (9 calories per gram).

Ratio—in relation to blood cholesterol; it is the relationship of your total cholesterol to your high density lipoproteins (HDLs) or stated another way, the total cholesterol divided by the HDLs. It is important for this ratio to be below certain levels. The higher the ratio is, the greater your risk of having a cardiovascular problem. For the least risk, men's ratio should be below four and women's below three.

Risk factor—trait or condition in a person that is associated with an increased chance (or risk) of developing a disease. When referring to the cardiovascular system, a risk factor is associated with an increased chance of having a heart attack or stroke.

Saturated fats—see fats.

Stroke—interruption of blood being supplied to a part of the brain through an artery which causes that area of the brain to be unable to function properly.

Thrombus—blood clot which forms inside a blood vessel or cavity of the heart; if a clot obstructs an artery in the heart, a heart attack may result; if it obstructs an artery going to the brain, a stroke may occur; if it obstructs a major leg artery, leg problems (pain, ulcers) may occur.

Triglycerides—lipids (fats) carried through the bloodstream to the tissues. The bulk of the body's fat tissue is in the form of triglycerides, stored for later use as energy. We get triglycerides primarily from the fat and extra calories in our diet.

Unsaturated fats—see fats.

Vascular—pertaining to the blood vessels.

Vascular disease—ailment of the blood vessels often caused by atherosclerosis. May occur in the arteries in the heart, arteries to the brain and the major leg arteries.

Veins—wide, thin-walled blood vessels which carry blood back from the body's tissues to the heart. They are divided into sections by valves that prevent the blood from flowing backward and allow the general muscular activity of the body to pump it toward the heart.

Very low density lipoproteins (VLDL)—see lipoproteins.

Handbook Index

Cookbook Index

OTHER PUBLICATIONS AVAILABLE FROM FRANKLIN PUBLISHERS

The following items may be ordered directly from Franklin Publishers, Box 1338, Bryn Mawr, PA 19010. Write for current prices.

- **THE LOW BLOOD SUGAR HANDBOOK**—by Edward and Patricia Krimmel. Highly praised by Harvey Ross, M.D., this is a new upscaled approach to the diagnosis and treatment of hypoglycemia (low blood sugar), written with the insight and practicality that only a sufferer could have, but backed up by meticulous research and medical accuracy. The book of solutions! 192 pages

- **THE LOW BLOOD SUGAR COOKBOOK**—by Patricia and Edward Krimmel. A very special collection of over 200 sugarless natural food recipes. Snacks to gourmet dishes designed specifically for the hypoglycemic, but which everyone can enjoy and are also valuable to diabetics and weight watchers. No artificial sweeteners or white flour are used in the recipes. Only fruit and fruit juices are used as sweeteners. 192 pages

- **ONE (1) HOUR LOW BLOOD SUGAR CASSETTE**
A dynamic presentation by the authors of THE LOW BLOOD SUGAR HANDBOOK, Ed & Pat Krimmel. Get the feeling of personal contact with the authors when hearing an interview followed by a question and answer session.

- **CHOLESTEROL LOWERING COOKBOOK**—by Patricia and Edward Krimmel. See page 118 or 248.

YEARLY UPDATE NEWSLETTER

As of September, 1990, you may receive current research information on cholesterol, including children and cholesterol. Send $10.00 and a self addressed, stamped business size envelope to Franklin Publishers. This is a yearly subscription.

ORDER YOUR COPY TODAY!

Mail payment with request for book(s). If paid by U.S. Postal Money Order, order will be mailed same day as received. Order three (3) or more copies and take a 10% discount. Use order form below if you wish. Publisher will pay mailing and handling costs. Pennsylvania residents, please add state sales tax.

Mail order to: Franklin Publishers
Box 1338, Bryn Mawr, PA 19010

ORDER FORM

CHOLESTEROL LOWERING AND CONTROLLING 3 WEEK PLAN: HANDBOOK & COOKBOOK

Send _____ copy(s), Cholesterol Lowering and Controlling 3 Week Plan: Handbook and Cookbook. Payment of $ _____ is enclosed. ($22.00 per book) 10% discount with order of 3 or more copies. No C.O.D. Canadian orders paid in U.S. dollars, Postal money order only. PA residents, include state sales tax.

(Please type or print)

Ship to:

Mr. / Mrs. _____

Address_____ APT. # _____

City _____ State _____ Zip _____

Phone (optional) Home _____ Bus. _____

YEARLY UPDATE NEWSLETTER

As of September, 1990, you may receive current research information on cholesterol, including children and cholesterol. Send $10.00 and a self addressed, stamped business size envelope to Franklin Publishers. This is a yearly subscription.

See previous page for additional publications by Franklin Publishers.